RISE
ABOVE

EMBRACING CHANGE, BUILDING RESILIENCE,
AND CULTIVATING CONNECTIONS

RISE ABOVE

EMBRACING CHANGE, BUILDING RESILIENCE, AND CULTIVATING CONNECTIONS

NILESH V. PATEL

Halo
PUBLISHING
INTERNATIONAL

Halo
PUBLISHING
INTERNATIONAL

Halo Publishing International
7550 WIH-10 #800, PMB 2069,
San Antonio, TX 78229

First Edition, September 2023
ISBN: 978-1-63765-391-3
Library of Congress Control Number: 2023904612

The information contained within this book is strictly for informational purposes. Unless otherwise indicated, all the names, characters, businesses, places, events and incidents in this book are either the product of the author's imagination or used in a fictitious manner. Any resemblance to actual persons, living or dead, or actual events is purely coincidental.

Halo Publishing International is a self-publishing company that publishes adult fiction and non-fiction, children's literature, self-help, spiritual, and faith-based books. We continually strive to help authors reach their publishing goals and provide many different services that help them do so. We do not publish books that are deemed to be politically, religiously, or socially disrespectful, or books that are sexually provocative, including erotica. Halo reserves the right to refuse publication of any manuscript if it is deemed not to be in line with our principles. Do you have a book idea you would like us to consider publishing? Please visit www.halopublishing.com for more information.

To my beloved parents and grandparents, who have inspired and empowered me through their way of life, which has been the foundation of my journey, I'm forever grateful.

CONTENTS

Section 2: Journey from Indian Village to the City Life

Section 3: Pursuit for a Better Future: Navigating the American Dream

Section 4: Cultural Crossroads in Japan: Connections, Work, and Celebration

Section 5: Discoveries in Japan: Success, Bonds, and Beyond

Introduction

Imagine growing up in India as a curious little boy, eagerly soaking up all the experiences and social interactions life has to offer. From exploring nature and animals, to playing with other children, you relished every moment. Your mischievous personality often caused headaches for your family and friends, but they showered you with love, affection, care, and support.

But at the start of adolescence, your world suddenly changed. You left behind all that was familiar and ventured to the Land of Opportunity, the United States, where you couldn't speak a word of English. Navigating unfamiliar cultural environments and social norms without much knowledge or support, you experienced emotional changes and the stress of leaving behind family, friends, and school in India. You went through a "silent period" as a kid, adapting to new environments and identities in a culture and school unknown to you.

Despite these challenges, you made the difficult changes, adjusted, and successfully graduated from high school and college. You landed a great job that took you far away from the United States to Japan, where you led a massive telecommunications-engineering project for one of the most iconic and best-managed companies in the country. Even though you were still improving your business communications and writing skills, you felt as if the universe were leading you somewhere and guiding you step-by-step through every challenge, anxious moment, and interaction with people.

As you traveled on business to Japan, you discovered your love for traveling and embracing different cultures and people. These experiences helped you not only to learn and grow, but also to see and appreciate your unique personality. You finally felt a part of everyone with whom you interacted and found inspiration and understanding behind those connections. You built and maintained lasting friendships with people from diverse backgrounds and cultures, which increased your sense of belonging and enriched your life.

As we embark on this transformative journey together, the pages of this book will unfold, revealing remarkable experiences, invaluable insights, and the power of human connection. Prepare to explore the myriad facets of life, from resilience and personal growth to cultural immersion and challenges that shape us. This extraordinary tale celebrates the tapestry of experiences, inviting you to be inspired, enlightened, and transformed by diverse perspectives and profound lessons that connect us all. So, turn the pages, unleash your imagination and discover more.

Section 1

Embracing Childhood, Tradition, and Unforgettable Memories in India

1. A Joyous Arrival: A Traditional Indian Birth Story

After my parents got married, my mother moved to my father's home in his village of Gujarat, along the western coast of India. They belonged to a traditional Indian joint family in which many generations live in the same house, bound by blood and marriage. As a child, I recall the house feeling as if it were a community, always packed with village people—such as uncles, aunts, cousins, and friends of my parents and grandparents—who frequently visited to drink chai. It was part of the village's hospitality and a social ritual in India.

When my mother was pregnant with me, it became increasingly challenging for her to manage the demanding daily tasks at my father's home in the village. Although my mother didn't work outside the home, she was busy all day with the household labor-intensive responsibilities, such as preparing meals, washing dishes and clothes by hand, and caring for my grandparents. Balancing these duties took a toll on her well-being. When the time came for her to enter the confinement period, a tradition still followed in many parts of India today, it provided a much-needed respite from her responsibilities. This period of confinement, observed by our ancestors, was designed to safeguard the health of both the mother and the baby, allowing for rest, recovery, and support from her own parents in the familiar surroundings of her childhood village.

Confinement—the tradition of young pregnant mothers moving back to their parents' homes and villages—is still followed in many parts of India today. Our ancestors initiated these practices to protect new mothers, keep babies healthy, and help new mothers recover from the exhaustion of childbirth. The confinement period came with many restrictions in food and movement for faster recovery.

Adhering to the confinement tradition of those days, my maternal grandmother invited my mother to live with her for a certain number of weeks before and after I was born. Based on the advice of her mother and aunts, my mother rested all day long and ate vegetarian meals specially prepared with herbs and natural ingredients by her mother and other female relatives. This way, as a new mother, she could regain her stamina, strength, and balance after delivery. It also served to reduce her stress, which could interfere with her milk supply for the baby and affect her well-being.

During this period, my father stayed in his home in the village. In those days, mobile phones didn't exist, and only the super-rich had phones in their homes in India. Letter delivery service was the most affordable means of long-distance communication, and letters were delivered quickly. So, my parents frequently used letters to communicate with each other while living in separate villages during the confinement period.

In the winter month of the new year, my mother wrote a letter to my father, asking him to meet her on a particular day at a known destination in the city of Vadodara, which was the largest and closest city to her village. My mother was expecting me any day and wanted to have a checkup at the doctor's office.

After an hour-long bus ride from their respective villages, they arrived separately in the city of Vadodara. Since they didn't have a car or motorcycle, the best local transportation for traveling between villages was a bus. They met at the known destination and took an auto-rickshaw, the local transportation available to them, to one of the best privately-owned maternity hospitals in Vadodara, where my parents really liked the highly skilled doctors and staff, special meals, and exceptional care for mothers and their newborn babies.

When my mother saw the doctor, he found everything normal and said, "The delivery of the baby could happen very soon." He suggested that she stay at the hospital until delivery if she wanted, but he couldn't predict the exact delivery date. However, my parents couldn't afford for my mother to stay in the hospital just waiting for the birth, as it was complicated and expensive. Instead, they pre-registered my mother and prepaid a ten-day stay at the hospital; that way, she was guaranteed a bed when she was ready to come back. They left the hospital, had a nice meal at a local restaurant they frequented, and each returned to their respective village homes the same evening.

The next day, my mother felt pressure and severe pain in her lower abdomen while resting at home in the evening. She communicated her condition to one of her younger sisters, who was with her. My grandmother was at the temple in the village where she regularly went for evening prayers; she was called home. Once my grandmother arrived, my mother's sister immediately asked a neighbor to fetch my grandfather, who was working at the family business, a grocery shop, that evening. He arrived and realized that my mother was in a lot of pain and needed immediate care and transport to the hospital in Vadodara. However, there was no bus scheduled for that evening from their village to Vadodara.

So, my grandfather's only option was to rent a bullock cart, a two-wheeled vehicle pulled by two bullocks, from a private owner. Villagers commonly used these carts for commuting and carrying goods since either modern vehicle were too expensive or the infrastructure didn't allow for any other mode of transportation. My grandfather arranged for the bullock cart to come to the main gate in the alleyway outside their home. The concerned neighbors saw my mother in severe pain while she was walking to where the bullock cart was waiting. The rider sat on the front of the bullock cart, while my mother and grandmother gently got in and sat in the back. As soon as they were seated, the cart proceeded towards the center of the village.

My grandmother realized that traveling to the nearest city, Padra, by bullock cart would take an incredibly long time, and then they would still need to take an auto-rickshaw to reach the hospital in Vadodara. She feared there might be an emergency in the middle of the road without lights at night. In those days, the single road that connected our village to Padra was rough and comprised of hard clay, unfinished pavement, and numerous large potholes. Traveling on this road posed a considerable challenge due to its poor condition and lack of proper infrastructure. Recognizing the difficulties that lay ahead, my grandmother asked my grandfather to see if the villagers could find alternative means of transportation. At that time, no one in our village owned a car since they were too expensive to own in India.

Under pressure and concerned for the health and safety of my mother, my grandfather quickly found a parked, full-size freight truck at the center of the village, where all the public buses stopped. He talked to the truck driver, who was elderly and lived in our village. He knew my grandfather very well. After being informed of the situation, the truck driver agreed to take my mother and grandmother to the nearest city, Padra, where they could then proceed by auto-rickshaw to Vadodara. Assuring my grandfather that he would, the truck driver pledged to take good care of them throughout the journey.

My mother and grandmother got in the front seat of the transport truck and sat squeezed together in an uncomfortable position on the single passenger seat. Freight trucks are not big in India. The seats are small, compared to the Mack trucks in the United States. However, my mother found a way to get comfortable, while my grandmother started praying. My mother didn't complain about pain during the rough, bumpy, and uncomfortable truck ride. She remained calm, kept a positive mindset throughout the ordeal, and dealt with whatever was happening with strength and determination.

Once they arrived in Padra, the truck driver generously offered to continue driving them all the way to the city of Vadodara, an hour-long ride. The truck driver was a kind elderly man; he told my grandmother he couldn't leave them waiting for public transportation on the side of the road. He dropped them off at the farthest point within the city that trucks were allowed.

They arrived in Vadodara on a cold night; the city was filled with vibrant sights and sounds. Its streets were adorned with colorful lights that illuminated the night, the lively atmosphere, crowd-filled markets, and busy street vendors and sidewalks. The aroma of street food filled the air with a delightful mix of Indian spices and flavors. The sounds of honking horns, laughter, melodic voices of street vendors, and Indian urban life offered my grandmother and mother a renewed sense of energy.

Before going to the hospital, my mother and grandmother took an auto-rickshaw to my grandmother's friend's home. She was delighted to see them and warmly welcomed them with a refreshing glass of chilled water and spicy home-made snacks. She also made hot, spiced ginger milk and a special herbal drink to comfort my mother. Afterward, my grandmother's friend decided to join them for guidance and support while my mother was admitted. The three of them went to the hospital in another auto-rickshaw. Hospital stays in those days were expected to be long, and there was no open cafeteria or place for family members to sleep in the patients' rooms. Therefore, waiting family members had to find a place to sleep in the hospital lobby, waiting areas, on benches, or in the homes of relatives or friends living near the hospital.

My mother registered herself quickly at the hospital, and the staff carefully took her to her assigned bed while my grandmother and her friend waited outside in the common waiting area. Late that night, past midnight, I was born, and it was a joyous moment for my mother, filled with overwhelming feelings of gratitude and happiness. When my grandmother heard the news, tears of joy filled with blessings flowed from her eyes; her friend's excitement was evident from the big smile on her face.

At the time of my birth, my father was away from our village, staying at his uncle's house in a different city for business training. My grandfather wrote him a letter to inform him of my arrival, and it took a couple of days for the message to reach him. As soon as he heard, he took a long train to Vadodara to see my mother and me. He was thrilled and relieved to see that we were both healthy.

When the news of my birth spread, a big celebration erupted in our homes back in our respective villages. My maternal grandparents distributed sweets, and my paternal grandparents distributed sugar candy, a family tradition to spread joy and happiness throughout the village for a newborn.

After ten days, my mother was discharged from the hospital and went back to her parents' home, where she continued the confinement practices for a couple more weeks. During that time, my father made frequent trips to visit my mother and me while we recovered. My grandparents and other extended family members from my father's side also visited us, bringing gifts and sweets.

When my mother was fully recovered, we went to my father's family's village, where she gradually started working most of the day and taking over household responsibilities, such as cleaning, cooking, and taking care of family affairs. Like other women in the village, she found some time every evening to visit with her friends and take nice long walks to the outskirts of the village. Her friends also had children, and they supported each other as new mothers, forming common bonds based on shared family values and commitments.

2. My Mothers' Life: Hard Work and Resilience

My mother's childhood taught her to be resilient in the face of challenges. Her remarkable attitude and unwavering faith helped her navigate the unexpected challenges she faced in the last days and hours of her first pregnancy. She had to move from the village to the city on bumpy bus rides, get in and out of the bullock cart, take an uncomfortable and noisy truck ride, change to an auto-rickshaw, and eventually become an inpatient at the hospital. The physical pain, emotional swings, changes in environment or situation, and mental stress required self-discipline, inner strength, and character. Despite everything, my mother remained calm and maintained a sense of confidence that everything would be all right.

My mother had faced unfamiliar and tough situations many times during her childhood and had always stayed positive, believing that something good would result from her ordeals. With this positive mindset, she remained focused on what she could control and didn't worry about what she couldn't. This way, she developed valuable skills to handle unexpected situations and endure uncertainty.

When my mother was between the ages of eight and sixteen, her mother (my grandmother) often fell sick and was away receiving medical treatments. Her mother also gave birth to her last two children during my mother's early teenage years. Following traditional confinement practices, her mother was away when confined to her parents' home before and after the birth of each child. My grandmother didn't have her in-laws living with her, as they had passed away. So, there were no experienced elderly women in the family who could assist pre- and post-pregnancy.

While my grandmother went to her village during the confinement period, my mother and her five younger sisters had to help manage household responsibilities. At this time, my grandfather also helped out at home as much as he could while still managing the family-owned grocery shop, farming, and attending family and social events in the village.

Every day, my mother woke up in the early morning hours and boiled water on a wood-burning, clay chulha for her bath. After bathing, she would make breakfast on the second chulha in the kitchen, while her father and other siblings took turns bathing. She usually made simple, local-style traditional Indian breakfasts that included whole wheat flatbread (parathas), flat rice chips, which were charcoal-roasted, spicy, tasty, and crispy. She made ginger-milk masala (chai) for her father and hot milk for her and her siblings. Her school hours were from 11:00 a.m. to 5:00 p.m., Monday through Friday, so she had plenty of time in the morning to take care of the household responsibilities.

At that time, they didn't have running water in the home, so they and the villagers relied on water from the water wells located in many parts of the village, usually within walking distance of their homes. To get water out of the well, they used iron, stainless steel, or plastic buckets attached to a rope or string. They also used the lake on the outskirts of the village for washing clothes by hand. This was a normal daily routine; the women in the village took care of household responsibilities, while the men went to work at their own businesses, for someone else, or on their farms.

After everyone finished bathing, my mother gathered up the dirty clothes and dishes from breakfast and carried them to the nearby lake for cleaning. Sometimes one of her younger sisters accompanied her to help, and her friends joined her to spend time together. After returning home, my mother swept the floors, both inside and outside the entrance, using a primitive broom made of delicate fibers and long, thin, dry grass. The washed clothes were hung to dry on a string or rope, either inside the home or on the rooftop terrace. Then my mother immediately started preparing lunch on the chulha, a traditional clay stove fueled by wood, coal, or dried cow-dung cakes commonly used in Indian village homes. She cooked most of the traditional Gujarati dishes from a young age. She sometimes went to manually milk their family-owned buffalo, a common practice among villagers for obtaining fresh milk. Most families in the village owned their own buffaloes for milk.

Amidst her busy schedule, my mother never neglected her responsibility to her younger sisters. She took the time to comb their hair, help them get dressed, and send them off to school before making her way to her own classes. After school, she returned home to fold the dry laundry and prepare dinner. If the household needed water, using iron buckets, she fetched it from the well. Her sisters also helped with some work at home or cooking whenever they were free. My mother's brother was also willing to help out with household tasks or other responsibilities when necessary, despite being younger than my mother and her sisters. After dinner, she cleaned up before spending time with her friends. They played, sang, and studied together, often accompanied by my mother's sisters.

Despite her many duties, my mother never grumbled about helping her family. In fact, she took pride in caring for her father and siblings while her mother was away. She always prioritized her responsibilities and schoolwork, even if it meant sacrificing some of her own free time.

When my mother visited her grandparents, uncles, and aunts in the city and villages, she was often asked to do unfamiliar tasks, such as cooking for large groups or assisting with farm work. She also offered guidance and helped her father with family affairs and the family-owned business. Though she wasn't always appreciated and sometimes faced rejection, these experiences gave her a deeper understanding of life and helped her develop people skills from an early age. As a result, she could manage relationships and handle situations easily and calmly in times of crisis, always taking others' feelings into consideration.

Despite her responsibilities, my mother had a playful personality during her childhood and teenage years. She loved to laugh, joke, and play pranks with her friends and the elders in the village. Athletics were also an important part of her identity, as she had always been athletic and strong, both mentally and physically. She played sports in school, ran regularly, and swam in the village lake.

When she got married young, she brought her strong character and playful nature into the union. As she grew older and became more true to herself, she realized the value of the lessons she'd learned from supporting her family and being active at home. These lessons helped her build character. My mother's journey through her childhood and teenage years in the village of India taught her also the value of hard work, resilience, self-discipline, and how to remain positive in the face of adversity and uncertainty. As a result, she faced unfamiliar and tough situations many times, but stayed positive and focused on what she could control as she developed valuable skills in handling unexpected situations. Through her experiences, she came to a deep understanding and perspective about life, which nurtured her blossoming personality and the deepening of her multiple virtues and values, setting the firm foundation of her authentic nature.

Despite facing physical pain, emotional swings, and mental stress during the last days and hours of her first pregnancy, my mother remained calm and maintained a sense of confidence that everything would be all right. This remarkable attitude and unwavering faith were a testament to the resilience she'd developed through the adversities of life.

My mother's story is an inspiration to many, and her experiences are a valuable reminder of the importance of hard work, perseverance, and a positive mindset in the face of life's challenges.

3. Village Life in India: Simple Joys and Timeless Traditions

It was a perfect morning during my childhood vacation with my mother in her village home outside of the city of Vadodara in Gujarat, India. I lay next to one of my aunts on a khatlo, a traditional Indian bed made of wood with white woven ropes. Some of the neighbors in the alley were sleeping outside like us. Other family members slept on the open rooftop. As the sun began to rise, I slowly opened my eyes, still feeling the remnants of sleep. The clouds gracefully parted, revealing the beauty of the morning sky. The serene morning atmosphere was filled with the crowing of roosters and the melodious songs of birds. As I cast my gaze down the alley, I noticed my neighbors quietly sitting outside their homes, enjoying the tranquility of the morning.

The air was infused with the fragrance of burning wood from the chulhas, the traditional stoves used for cooking and boiling water on stainless steel containers. Some neighbors were heating water in buckets on their chulhas for their morning showers. Meanwhile, adults and children alike were seen outside, brushing their teeth or eagerly waiting for their refreshing cups of freshly made chai or hot milk, as well as a warm traditional breakfast consisting of whole wheat flatbread (parathas), flattened rice flakes (poha), and a variety of dry snacks. The local children were preparing for school, their youthful energy filling the air with excitement. In some homes, the uplifting morning-devotional songs known as pabhatiyas were playing on the radio, inspiring listeners and filling their hearts with positivity, setting the perfect tone for a wonderful day ahead. Once my aunt awakened, I eagerly assisted her in folding bed sheets and blankets and carrying our pillows. Afterwards, she gracefully hung the khatlo, our cherished traditional Indian bed, on a hook in the front balcony wall.

My grandmother strongly emphasized the practice of showering and praying before eating, which was deeply ingrained in our family culture and tradition. It was a ritual we followed diligently, respecting its significance. With multiple family members living together, we took turns showering one at a time. The morning routine started with my grandmother being the first to wake up, take an early shower, and engage in her prayers. Meanwhile, one of my aunts stepped outside with a stainless steel container and a stool to tend to our family-owned buffalo, which was kept outside our home at a designated area. She provided a nourishing wheat mix and fresh grass to the buffalo and then manually milked it to obtain fresh milk for our family's consumption. This practice of showering, praying, and tending to the buffalo was an integral part of our daily routine. Many villagers followed similar traditions.

After showering, I joined my aunts, uncle, and grandfather for morning prayers. Then my grandmother or one of my aunts made spiced ginger-milk chai and hot, spiced ginger milk and traditional homemade snacks. Most of us had breakfast together on the floor. My grandfather and uncle then made a quick visit to the temple, which was within walking distance, before going to open the family-owned grocery store.

After my youngest aunt left for school, one of my other aunts at home swept the floor, while another loaded the dirty clothes in a large tin container, put it on her head, and with a small bucket and wooden washing paddles, went to the village lake to hand-wash the clothes with the other village women. Since the village didn't have running water all day long, this was the only way to do the wash, and it was a normal way of life for the villagers. While the washing was being done, my grandmother or one of my aunts started preparing lunch. All the day's chores were done routinely and quickly; everyone at home had assigned responsibilities and knew who was to do what and when. Once the chores were done, then everyone went about their business.

Spending summer vacations during my childhood at my maternal grandmother's village home, I discovered a profound sense of belonging deep in the embrace of timeless Indian traditions and the rhythm of family life. It was there that I witnessed the beauty of simplicity and found joy in the everyday moments that shaped our days. I feel incredibly grateful to have had the chance to immerse myself in these precious and cherished traditions of village life in India.

4. A Glimpse into Indian Village Life: Joyful Memories

Sometimes, my friends and I went to our farm in my mother's village or the farm of one of my friends and played around the trees, picking different types of locally grown fruits, or climbing a tree and sitting there for a little bit to talk. Our common choice was going to my grandparents' farm, especially during the summer months when the mango season was in full swing and eating freshly squeezed mangoes right off the trees. But to do that, we had to walk a long way. My grandfather had a really nice, small, hut-size place to rest on our farm, so we went there to sleep and play different games.

We often enjoyed watching the farm workers as they sowed, managed, or picked crops. Whenever they noticed us playing, they smiled and kept a watchful eye on us to ensure we didn't get hurt while climbing the trees. They were always so generous in taking care of me and my friends while we played, even offering us clean water that they had brought from home in clay pots. Some of my village friends knew of a nearby water pump used to provide water to the farms, so we occasionally went there for fresh water. When the heat at the farm became unbearable, we cooled off by diving into the nearby waterfall or using water hoses to take a refreshing shower on a humid day.

I also caused some harmless mischief for my aunts and neighbors. One of my favorite pastimes was chasing after goats or cows that belonged to someone else, much to my amusement and that of my friends. We laughed heartily as the owners yelled at us as they tried to round up their animals.

Often, while playing in the village, we encountered close relatives. In these instances, extended family members usually greeted me warmly, invited me to their homes and offered me candy, biscuits, or other snacks while inquiring about the well-being of my parents and other family members. I enjoyed these chance encounters so much that, when my friends and I walked by their homes, I often stopped and knocked on their doors to say hello to whoever was inside. If they were outside, then I stood and talked with them for a few minutes. This habit of mine became so well-known that news of my visits to family members' homes quickly spread. They were excited to see me. It was a pleasant way to pass the time in the village. The people were always modest, humble, happy, and loving. Even though some didn't have a lot of money or large homes, they were always welcoming, willing to help, and smiling. I never saw a lot of fights or arguments among them.

If I got hungry, I went home for lunch, but if not, I stayed outside with my friends until dusk. When I didn't show up for a meal, my family assumed I was all right and wouldn't be coming home until late. The village was surrounded by lush farms, which we loved to explore with our friends. Sometimes, we even ventured into the farms and picked fresh fruits or vegetables to satisfy our hunger. We also occasionally stumbled upon a tomato or sweet potato field. It was always exciting to explore the farms and discover new things to eat. We enjoyed the feeling of independence that came with being able to find our own food.

Sometimes, I saw my grandmother and aunts using a traditional method to make homemade fresh butter and buttermilk. In India, buttermilk, locally known as chaas, is a popular beverage consumed during meals to help keep the body cool in hot climates, and it's also healthy. It's made by diluting yogurt with water and adding various spices, herbs, and salt to enhance the flavor.

They used a special wooden machine called a butter churn, which has been used for centuries in India to make butter and buttermilk from milk. The butter churn consisted of a wooden paddle, placed on a heavy clay pot, used to agitate the milk and cream inside. This process transformed the mixture into buttermilk or butter. The churning required two people to turn the paddle back and forth, so I always tried to help and participate in the fun. I loved the sound of the machine creaking as it churned the milk, and the delicious aroma of freshly made butter that filled the room.

My grandparents owned a buffalo, as most villagers did, to produce milk at home. Homemade butter and buttermilk had a unique and tasty flavor and texture that made them truly special.

In addition to making butter, I also enjoyed watching my grandmother and aunts prepare homemade sweets and snacks, such as my favorite peda, a traditional Indian sweet made with milk, sugar, and nuts, as well as crispy samosas filled with spicy potatoes. They patiently taught me the recipes and showed me how to mix the ingredients, roll the dough, and fry the snacks. This time spent together in the kitchen was a great bonding experience with the maternal side of my family, and I cherished every moment of it.

Monkeys were always hanging out by our homes. It was normal to see monkeys on the rooftops of people's homes in India. Occasionally, in search of food, the monkeys attempted to enter our kitchen through its large open window. The scent of spices and cooked food wafting out of the kitchen attracted them, and we had to act quickly to scare them away with a wooden stick before they got too close to us or the food in the kitchen. Other times, they simply sat on the rooftops and stared at us with their curious eyes, so we offered them bananas or some peanuts. They would either run away, or we chased them away, and watched their tails swaying behind them as they fled.

After the evening meal, I often had the opportunity to spend time with various family members. Sometimes, I joined my aunts on visits to their friends, or accompanied my grandmother to the women-only temple for evening prayers. Other times, I joined my uncle or grandfather while they visited their friends in the village. It was always fascinating to meet new people and learn about their lives, and I cherished these moments spent with my elders in the family.

The daily routine in the village was consistent, but it was also lively, active, and filled with joy. I felt a strong sense of belonging. Everyone lived in a joint family, and people of all ages, whether rich or poor, coexisted harmoniously. I stayed busy throughout the day, playing games, attending prayers, visiting farms, socializing, and spending time with adults. This allowed me to reconnect with myself after spending most of the year attending school in the city, where the life-style and people were vastly different from those in the village. It was this balance of spending time with my grand-parents, aunts, uncles, their friends, family members, and my village friends that allowed me to remain true to my identity, stay connected to my roots, and appreciate the simplicity and beauty of rural life in India.

5. Memories of Scorching Bus Rides and Sweet Mangoes

As a child, I eagerly awaited the end of the school year, not just for the break from studies but for the annual summer vacations to the remote villages of my maternal and paternal grandparents in Gujarat, India. These villages embodied the traditional charm of India and provided me with unforgettable experiences, moments of learning, and a chance to develop my passions. The joint families of both grandparents welcomed me with open arms, and I relished the opportunity to bond with my uncles, aunts, and cousins. Every summer was filled with endless fun and exploration that I still treasure today.

As soon as the bell rang on the final day of the school year, I could hardly contain my excitement to escape the city of Vadodara and embark on my annual summer adventure in the villages. My mother, sister, and I rode to the villages on a public bus, while my father stayed back in the city. The journey to my maternal grandparents' remote village was long and bumpy, while the hot summer sun that beat down upon us. With one major stop where we had to transfer to another bus to reach our final destination, Seeing the vibrant roads and streets from the city to the village filled with people on foot, bicycles, auto-rickshaws and scooters. Street-food vendors selling delicious treats and ice chilled water and refreshing beverages, providing a much-needed reprieve from the scorching hot Indian summer temperatures.

We watched the crowded public buses and heavily loaded trucks zoom past. Despite the discomfort and dehydration that came with the ride, we eagerly awaited our arrival at the first major bus stop, where we could quench our thirst with cold water from the closest street vendor, who usually was standing under an umbrella wearing a lightweight, multicolored hat to protect from the hot sun.

The hardships of the journey were quickly forgotten once we reached our destination, replaced by a sense of joy and anticipation. As we stepped foot outside the bus into the village, the air was filled with happiness to see my friends, maternal grandparents and relatives, with the palpable passion of my grandfather's passion for maintaining the family's mango tradition each year. So, we welcomed the summer with open arms, eagerly awaiting the sweet mangoes that were a symbol of abundance and the timeless bond of love.

6. Memories of Mangoes: My Grandfather's Legacy

Growing up in India, summer was always a special time of year for me. This was when it was mango season, and some mangoes had ripened and some were ready to ripen on the trees under the scorching sun, prompting my maternal grandfather to prepare to bring them home for us to eat. Mangoes played a significant part in our family culture, and their arrival was celebrated uniquely and memorably.

In the village, my grandfather owned a small family grocery store that served the local people, as well as a small farm where he grew vegetables for local markets. On his farm, he had some mango trees, the fruit from which he either sold in his shop or at the local market or brought them home. A worker who lived on the farm with his family helped him manage the daily farming responsibilities and took care of the crops, while my grandfather focused the majority of his time on managing the grocery store. He also received assistance from his son, my uncle, whenever he was home from college in the city.

My grandfather used a bicycle to travel around the village and commute to the grocery store. He was a tall, handsome, light-skinned man who wore traditional Indian clothing, a white dhoti and kurta. He was a family man, and he took care of his responsibilities. He often took me with him to visit his friends in their homes and to see the village elders with whom he had built long-lasting relationships. Everyone knew each other in the village. It was during those times I learned his character and observed the skills he had developed in managing relationships, interacting with people, and handling business affairs.

As I observed my grandfather in action, I saw a man with intelligence, strong character, and humility. He took pleasure in living a simple life and believed it his responsibility to do what was right and appropriate, regardless of others' opinions. When I closely watched, reflected upon, and learned from his daily activities and affairs, I realized that my grandfather had a clear vision for his future. He was acutely aware of his surroundings, and I came to admire his attitude, commitment to doing the right thing, self-confidence in pursuing opportunities, and love and passion for serving others. He was deeply spiritual and never compromised his values and faith. He treated everyone with respect, regardless of their background or income level.

My grandfather had years of experience in harvesting mangoes and knew the perfect time to pick them from the trees. He was skilled at hiring workers and effectively communicated their responsibilities and his plans for the mangoes. However, when it came to making advance deals for varieties of other sweet mangoes that were not grown on our farm, he negotiated with other farmers from the village to make advance deals and ensure we had an ample supply of the popular varieties of mangoes, usually enough to fill a living-room-sized room, for our home throughout the season.

My grandfather instructed his workers to pick and collect fully matured mangoes immediately, including those that had fallen from the trees. They used their hands if they could reach the mangoes from the ground, or a long mango picker to reach the mangoes if they were out of reach.

After the workers had gathered enough mangoes to fill up a large mesh bag, they tightly tied it and informed my grandfather of the number of collected mangoes and bags. He then delegated a worker from his grocery store to look after it for a couple of hours while he arranged to transport the mangoes from our farm to our home. He rode his bicycle in the hot, blazing sun to the center of the village where all the four-wheeled, wooden mobile cart owners would be waiting to transfer things manually by foot. He then found a suitable cart owner to deliver the mangoes. Since no one had a mobile phone in those days, everything was arranged in person. My grandfather gave the cart owner the location of our farm to pick up mesh bags and deliver them to our home. To ensure prompt and reliable delivery, my grandfather paid the cart owner up-front so they could make the trip to our farm and back.

7. The Sweet Taste of Tradition of Mangoes in Summer

In anticipation of our arrival in the village, during the weeks before my summer break from school, my grandfather started planning ahead for these large quantities of raw mangoes to be delivered for us at home. He set up a special room, usually on the second floor, in which the harvested mangoes were allowed to fully ripen. He would have the room mopped with clean water, and the floor was covered with a special cloth, over which a layer of straw was laid to provide a nest for the mangoes. Seeing the room prepared for the mangoes was always a sign that the season was approaching, and the excitement would begin.

Once the mangoes arrived, they were handled gently, as they can bruise easily, and laid on the straw, one mango at a time. They were basically lined up perfectly, vertically and horizontally; then they were covered with more straw, atop which a large mesh cloth was laid. Then the mangoes were left to sit for some days under natural conditions. During this time, the summer temperature rose very high, and the humidity levels increased, which created the ideal conditions for the mangoes to ripen.

The mangoes ripened very well in the high temperature. We weren't allowed to go in the room until they were fully ripe and ready to eat. However, every time I went to the second floor and passed by the mango room, I could smell their sweet, fruity aroma. The more they ripened, the more fragrant the odor that seeped through the double doors of the mango room. We slept in rooms close to the mango room, so we smelled them all through the night while sleeping.

Because of my mischievous nature, I always snuck into the mango room while they were ripening; the door was kept unlocked. I liked to see them with my own eyes, feel them, admire the vibrant colors, and smell them. I couldn't eat any of them because everybody at home would know about the yellow stain on my face or on my clothes. I was wary of getting caught, but that didn't prevent me from taking a risk once in a while and eating one or two fully ripe, delicious, fresh mangoes before everyone else had a chance to do the same.

When the time came to eat the mangoes, we all gathered —my grandparents and everyone in the family, including the kids—and were so happy to make the first freshly squeezed mango pulp. This was done in a large pot, and it was eaten alone or with food. Once the first batch of mangoes was finished, my grandfather would have the second and third batches delivered. We continued eating mangoes all summer, until there were no more mangoes on our farm or in the market.

This tradition of bringing mangoes home, waiting for them to perfectly ripen, and eating them is the most memorable thing about my childhood. Even today, we celebrate the same way, buying quality mangoes in boxes, waiting for them to ripen, making handmade fresh pulp using a blender, and eating it with ghee (purified butter), ginger powder, double-layer roti (wheat flatbread), and other food items. But today's methods cannot compare to experiencing hundreds of mangoes in a single room, layered on a floor, ripe and ready to eat; or to inhaling their natural aroma anytime you walked into the room. It was just more fun to pick a mango, eat it with your hands, and have stained fingers and mess all around my mouth and on my clothes. Mangoes kept all of us bonded and made us happier together.

Years have passed since my grandfather's death, but his memory and legacy continue to thrive in our family. Although the small family-owned grocery store he used to run has been sold, the building still stands as a testament to his hard work and dedication. Although the farm was sold, we still fondly recall the days of harvesting and enjoying mangoes during our summer vacations. Whenever I see a mango or taste its sweet, tangy flavor, I'm reminded of my childhood memories with my grandfather. His love for mangoes wasn't just about the fruit, but about the process of growing and harvesting them, and the joy that they brought to our family. It's a tradition that has been passed down through generations and will always hold a special place in my heart.

I feel grateful to have had the privilege of experiencing this rich tradition on both sides of my family. It's thanks to the dedication of both my grandfathers that we celebrated this tradition.

8. King of Fruits: Mango Pickle Frenzy

Making mango pickles was just as important for family bonding as our family tradition of eating a large variety of juicy mangoes. My childhood summer vacations always coincided with the arrival of raw mangoes. The local vegetable and fruit markets were flooded with green, raw mangoes, and street vendors with their carts got busy selling a variety of mangoes specifically cultivated for making authentic home-made achar (pickles).

My maternal grandmother and mother made traditional sweet, sour, and spicy mango pickles. I remember going with them to the wholesale markets, searching for dark-green, large, oval-shaped mangoes strictly used for pickles. These raw mangoes were difficult to handle and dangerous to grate into thin strips or cube-shaped pieces. It required a special skill, which my mother and grandmother possessed.

Depending on where I was staying at the time, making mango pickles was an annual summer tradition that both my mother and grandmother followed. They often helped each other, and even my aunts got involved. All the women collected the ingredients and mixed the spices ahead of time. They talked, drank milk tea, ate snacks, and helped one another. I was always eager to join in the frenzy, delighting in the first taste of raw mangoes or just playing around.

Cutting the mangoes was the hardest part. A special heavy-duty chopper or utensil was used to grate the mangoes, and both were very sharp and dangerous if not handled carefully. My maternal grandfather and father always found themselves in the middle of this craze. I observed with focused attention and learned from my grandfather while he was helping my grandmother chop fat mangoes into small, cube-shaped pieces. In the same way, my father helped my mother grate raw mangoes into thin shreds.

For sweet pickles, the entire mango skin was removed by hand using a sharp vegetable peeler, which made the mangoes slippery and hard to grip. With a hard grip, single-directional, long strokes are made down the mango's sides, producing even-shaped strips.

For sour and spicy pickles, the skin was left on the mango, and the entire mango, down to the hard, thick pit in the middle, was chopped into cube-sized pieces. I often assisted my grandmother and mother in the mango-pickling process.

Once the mangoes were chopped, the pieces were placed in thick ceramic jars. The pickling juice, along with the mixed spices and other ingredients that had already been prepared by the women, was poured over the chopped mangoes until the jars were full. These ceramic pots were sealed and then stored in a cool place or refrigerated. It took about a week for the mangoes to become pickled and ready to eat after soaking up all the mixed ingredients and spices. We used those pickles with a variety of dishes and in different ways all year long.

The whole process was incredible to watch and experience—the concentrated smell of the natural mix of pickling spices, the taste of the homemade pickles, and the rich custom from the roots and genuine artistry of many generations. I have vivid memories of infinite childhood summers in India, the kitchen filled with grandparents, parents, and aunts, all involved in helping one another pickle the mangoes.

Sometimes my mother packed parathas (wheat flatbreads), and sweet pickles in my plastic school lunch box. I always paired up with my friends at lunchtime, and we sat and shared our food. They loved my mother's delights, so I always asked her to pack extra to share with my friends.

9. Exploring Village Life with Friends

Some of my fondest childhood memories were spent with my friends in the scorching heat at my maternal grandparents' farm during the summer months' holidays. Like any kid, I couldn't wait to have fun and play. Each day, I was excited about spending time with my friends before I even had breakfast. I daydreamed about all the activities we could do together that day. For me, village life was a playground, and having friends around made it even more enjoyable. It allowed me to spend quality time with them and connect on a personal level, which helped me gain a broader perspective on life. We explored and experienced different types of exciting village activities and cultures that were much different from those in Vadodara, the city where we lived in the state of Gujarat. Even at that young age, I knew that these experiences would help us become closer.

As a playful child, I was always on the lookout for unique, fun things to do with my friends. When my friends suggested different activities, I was inspired and eager to participate. Back then, there was little fear of the unknown because we were confident that we would have fun no matter what we did. If we got into trouble, we would support each other and succeed together. However, village life was slower paced than city life, so I had to learn to be patient and adapt.

The sense of community and connectedness in the village was truly remarkable, especially when compared to the more isolated and individualistic lifestyle in the city. Everyone, from the elders to the children, interacted with one another throughout the day. They lived modest lives and showed great care and respect in their relationships with each other. When someone needed to borrow a few household items, such as milk, sugar, rice, lentils, or cooking oil, the neighbors were always there to help out. Women went to each other's houses to assist with cooking or share recipes, while the men gathered outdoors to engage in lively and passionate discussions on various topics, like politics, sports, and social issues.

The women also gathered every week at different homes to celebrate and sing traditional religious devotional songs, while the men had casual conversations with each other. The atmosphere was always filled with laughter, jokes, and heated debates, and it was clear that these gatherings were an important part of their social lives. The village lifestyle provided a unique opportunity to foster close relationships and create a strong sense of community.

The entire village felt as if it were one big family. When someone faced challenges, the rest of the villagers gathered around them in support. Everyone trusted one another; it felt as if almost anything could be shared with your neighbors who were always available to guide and mentor those facing difficulties, provide stability, safety, a supportive mindset, and friendliness during life's ups and downs.

Villagers maintained constant communication with friends, family members, and neighbors throughout the day, which was crucial for building and maintaining productive personal relationships. Good communication and attention to detail kept them productive and satisfied and minimized stress. Although villagers struggled to earn a better living, their overall life was happier, more content, and healthier than that of city dwellers who had more tangible wealth. My friends were from small village families with limited income and resources, but they were always welcoming, warm, modest, and simple people who made me feel proud to be part of their journey.

I remember one perfect, clear, hot day when we gathered at the outskirts of the maternal village before embarking on a long walk to the farm. It was during the Indian summer months, and we were expecting a blazing sun that afternoon. Despite the heat, I was dressed casually in a short-sleeved, half-buttoned shirt, full-cotton shorts, and slippers. The village was bustling with people on foot, bicycles, scooters, and motorcycles. In the center of the village stood a huge tree, one of the oldest in the area.

Underneath that tree, elderly men sat on stone benches, engaged in sociable conversations with their friends. Many of them read daily newspapers, while some had their grandchildren with them. The street vendors with their wooden mobile carts were always busy selling food and vegetables.

In the area there were girls' and boys' schools where kids were playing outside in the schoolyards, while in some classrooms, teachers were engrossed in serious educating as students focused on their studies. There was also a towering concrete water tank, and in front of it was a small village-government administrative office. The area had a couple of small grocery stores with loudspeakers blaring local folk music in order to grab the attention of passersby. These shops sold essential items, such as groceries, vegetable oil, cookies, candies, snacks, and tobacco products.

In the corner of the area, there was a small lake where some women were washing clothes by hand, while some children happily swam or took baths with plastic buckets while standing on the large stone steps. There were many different styles of small mud homes where people with lower levels of income lived, most of whom were agricultural workers. Some families had lived there for generations, and they warmly smiled at us as we passed by.

My friends and I walked closely together, enjoying each other's company and making the most of every moment by joking, laughing, teasing, and chatting. The narrow dirt road leading to the farm was long, and the ground was scorching hot. We couldn't stand barefoot for very long. I wore slippers with rubber soles, but they did little to ease the heat from the dirt. While walking, my slippers became soft, and I could feel the hot dirt and small rocks through my shoes, causing blisters to form on the bottoms of my feet. Like my friends, I didn't have proper shoes to wear on the rough dirt roads. I only had one good pair of shoes that my parents could afford, which I wore only on special occasions, such as weddings, family parties, or when I was invited as a guest to someone's home.

As we walked, the rugged terrain was a constant challenge, littered with gravel, scattered broken pieces of small glass, loose natural materials, plastic, rubber, nails, paper, used bags, and rocks. After rain, it wasn't uncommon to be splattered with mud kicked up by passing bicycle riders or motorcyclists. We also had to be cautious of farmers riding in bullock carts and farm workers or shepherds guiding sheep, goats, and cattle. Sometimes, we couldn't resist the temptation of chasing the sheep or goats away from their keepers, causing the herders to yell and scream at us and run around with long wooden sticks. As we journeyed on, we sometimes stumbled upon people manually milking their privately owned buffaloes in open fields on their own farms or at their homes.

Resting in cool shade was a welcome relief from the scorching heat, and we cherished those respites. We played games, like Antakshari, a traditional Indian singing game, or Lagori, a game where we stacked small stones and knocked them down with a ball. We also shared stories, jokes, and riddles, just generally enjoying each other's company.

Some of us dozed off; the sound of rustling leaves and singing birds lulled some of us to sleep. After taking a quick power nap, we gathered our energy, stretched our legs, and continued our journey towards the farm, looking forward to the fresh air, open fields, and cool breeze that awaited us.

When we became hungry during the walk to the farm, we were able to find various types of amazing tropical fruits that we could pick by hand from the trees. These fruits were unique to the region and very popular with the locals. Some of the fruits we enjoyed included java plums, jujubes, custard apples, wood apples, khirnis, camachiles, phalsas, bilberries, blackberries, and guavas. Not only are they delicious, but these seasonal fruits of India are also packed with essential nutrients and health benefits.

Gujarat, the western state of India where we lived, is the largest producer of fruit in India. For the local people, it's a natural pastime to indulge in the unique and rare Indian fruits that I used to love eating every day while in the village. These fruits grew freely and were easy to find while walking to the farm. We picked them by hand or used small stones from the ground to bring down the ripe, vibrantly colored fruits, which were always ready to eat.

We continued to seek out other options to satisfy our hunger, and ripe mangoes with their vibrant hues of red, orange, and yellow were an obvious choice. However, these trees were typically located deeper within the farm's land, making them more difficult to access due to the fenced borders that were designed to keep out unwanted predators. Despite the challenge, we persevered, jumping over the fence, searching for a way to sneak under it, or scouting for an opening to slip through.

Once we managed to get inside the fenced area, we quickly scanned the trees for ripe mangoes, only targeting the fully ripe ones with vibrant colors. If we could reach them by hand, we plucked them gently, but if they were out of our reach, we used small stones to hit the top of the stems where they were attached to the branches of the trees. It required skillful aim, as a misstep could rupture the mango and make it inedible. Once we had the mangoes, we retreated to a large tree and hid there while relishing the juicy fruit, trying not to get caught.

Once we got to the farm, my friends and I always made sure to introduce ourselves to the workers and explain why we were at the farm. They were living on the farm to protect it and its crops, often with their families. Once the workers recognized me, they were overjoyed and asked about everyone at home. The farm workers were incredibly hospitable, offering us a place to sit, homemade food cooked on charcoal clay stoves in their huts, and fresh, clean water from a clay pot that kept it cool. They even insisted that we rest for a little bit on their woven-rope, wooden-framed beds, which were placed in shaded areas under a tree or inside their huts. They wanted to ensure that we didn't get sick from the heat while playing in the sun all day long.

After resting for a while, we excitedly explored the farm, playing games and enjoying each other's company. The farm had incredible rope swings hanging from sturdy tree branches, handmade by the workers for their own children. It was a delightful experience swinging on them. The workers were kind enough to provide us with tips on how to climb the mango trees safely and avoid falling off, and they also offered us advice on how to pick the perfectly ripe mangoes.

Sometimes, while climbing mango trees, we came across monkeys perched on the branches, either resting or sleeping with their heads down. Monkeys have a fondness for mangoes, and often entire families, including babies can be found in the trees. They played, jumped around, and even fought with each other. Some of them preferred to stay on a single tree, while others quickly moved to the next one. If we encountered a large group of monkeys, we scared them off by screaming loudly or pretending to hold something in our hands. These intelligent creatures then moved to a nearby safe area. Once they were gone, we resumed eating mangoes and left them alone. Eating mangoes in the trees while feeling the cool breeze of nature and listening to birdsong was a delightful experience.

My friends and I spent hours on the farm, savoring its fruits, having fun, and exploring everything it had to offer. We got lost in a maze, sat under a tree, tromped around in a big open area full of hay, climbed, jumped, and played. Experiencing the natural way of life on the farm was incredibly peaceful.

As the hot and humid day neared its end, my friends showed me a nearby water-pump facility that provided water to the farms in the area. To help us cool down, we went there to drink clean, fresh running water and take a quick bath using the water hose.

Reflecting on these childhood memories of time spent with friends in the village, I'm filled with gratitude for the experiences that shaped my outlook on the world. Spending time in the village exposed me to people of different cultures and economic backgrounds, and interacting with them helped me develop a sense of empathy and understanding for diverse living. Through these experiences, my perspective on life broadened, and I gained a deeper appreciation for the value of community building, simplicity, and friendship.

10. A Wooden Swing and Afternoon Naps

My maternal grandparents' home was a beautiful three-story, brick-and-concrete building with a front porch and stone walkway; it was built on the village's high ground. The main entrance had custom wooden double doors that complemented the style of the home. All the flooring was of heavily designed tiles. The first floor had a large, open kitchen window in the back. It was big enough that we could look out the window and see all kinds of people and the local street activities. Occasionally we saw the villagers' traditional Indian wedding celebrations as they passed the house.

The second floor of the home had a wide balcony at the back over a partial sheet-metal roof, while the third floor had a similar setup with a large concrete terrace in the front. The house had all the basic amenities, and overhead water tank to store water and an area for clean drinking water.

One of my fondest memories of my grandparents' home is the specially wood-crafted, rectangular, polished swing attached to the ceiling in the middle room on the first floor. It was a place of great joy and playfulness for me and my friends. We took turns going fast, back and forth, trying to touch our feet to the ceiling. The room was a peaceful place, but it was darker than the other rooms, so it was lit by a fluorescent tube.

The swing wasn't only a fun place to play, but it was also a comfortable place for an afternoon power nap, a very common practice in India among people of all backgrounds, genders, professions and labors. From saints and scholars, to taxi and auto-rickshaw drivers. The short afternoon nap is one of the oldest Indian traditions, and that swing was the perfect place to take one.

Today, we are beginning to become aware of the benefits of short power naps in the afternoon for people of all ages. Many governments and medical experts encourage people to power nap. It can make a huge difference in people's health and well-being. Many companies around the world are adding sleep spaces for naps to their plans to provide an encouraging and supportive work environment. They are allowing and encouraging their employees to take these naps, which have proven to boost employees' energy, creativity, efficiency, and problem-solving abilities, while reducing stress.

My grandparents' home wasn't only a beautiful place, but also a place of comfort and relaxation, especially with the wooden swing in the middle room. It served as a reminder of the importance of taking a break to boost our energy, creativity, efficiency, and problem-solving abilities while reducing stress. As I reflect on my memories of swinging on that wooden swing, I'm grateful for my grandparents' home and the valuable life lessons it taught me.

11. The Mean Buffalo Who Became My Friend

As a kid growing up, I spent many happy summer vacations in my maternal grandparents' village, where I played with friends and created cherished memories. Over the years, some of these childhood friends have become more than just friends; they are now integral parts of my life.

One of these friends came from a family with a long history of farming. They owned a large farm on which there were buffalo and oxen. The buffalo provided milk, while the oxen were used for plowing the fields or pulling carts for transportation. To me, these animals represented the epitome of hard work and strength. Even today, farmers in India rely on buffalo and oxen in their daily work.

My friend always invited me to spend time playing and hanging out on his family's farm. His family had built a small hut next to a grove of large trees that provided shade from the hot sun. The hut was made of the most popular building materials in Indian villages: bricks and natural clay. These materials helped to keep the hut cool during the hot summers. The hut's roof, however, was sheet metal.

The farm mainly grew vegetables, such as tomatoes and eggplants, as well as fruits, like bananas and mangoes. The hut was a perfect place for family members to live during the harvesting period and to look after the crops. Workers occasionally ate and drank water inside it or rested in it during the afternoon after a long day of working in the heat and humidity of the summer months.

Protecting the farm from outside animals and people trying to steal was also a serious challenge. Deterring animals, like deer and monkeys, from entering the fields was part of the job for those working or staying on the farm. My friend's family and the farm workers spent a lot of their time protecting the farm from outside threats.

We spent our days in the open field on the farm, playing and enjoying the beauty of nature. We ran, jumped on piles of hay, and climbed trees. We ate delicious, freshly picked vegetables, such as tomatoes, cucumbers, eggplants, and okra, and even lemons with salt.

One day, while visiting my friend's farm, I noticed a group of buffaloes tied to a large tree with long iron chains. They were standing or sitting peacefully, constantly chewing on grass. One of the buffaloes stood out among the group. All of them were black, but this one buffalo was very strong, muscular, and fierce. Every time I went near or passed, it widened its nostrils and exhaled long, heavy breaths with a mean and intimidating look. It didn't allow other buffaloes to enter its territory. It looked gentle at times, but it had sharp horns and wasn't afraid to make an aggressive move when anyone came near.

Only a select few people in my friend's family were allowed to be near the mean buffalo when it needed to be fed, cared for, or milked. However, as a daily routine, all of the buffaloes were let out into the open field to roam and eat grass in their natural habitat. Sometimes, they were taken to a nearby small lake to drink or cool themselves in the water.

As I made more trips to the farm, I grew to love that buffalo. One hot and humid day, my friend and I were walking behind or beside the buffaloes, trying to handle them as if we were a small herd. I soon grew tired, felt dehydrated, and began having trouble walking. We stopped at a local water-pump station that distributed clean water to the farms so that I could drink some water and rest under a tree to protect myself from the blazing sun. After a short break, we continued walking.

During our frequent stops, the buffaloes began to spread out in the open field. Before we knew it, my friend and I were way behind them, so we tried to walk faster to catch up. When I neared the mean buffalo, it approached me as if it knew how I was feeling. It sensed that I was struggling to walk, getting tired, and feeling weak. Although I was afraid of its sharp horns and aggressive nature, I could tell that it was curious about me.

From a distance, my friend saw what was happening and the playfulness of the buffalo trying to get close to me. He loudly screamed, "Jump on; sit on the buffalo."

At first, I didn't understand what the buffalo was trying to convey, and I was too scared to get too close. I thought my friend was out of his mind. But after my friend encouraged me to jump on the buffalo, he eventually came over and lifted me onto the animal.

Sitting uncomfortably on the buffalo and feeling scared, I asked my friend to stay close to me. I'd never sat on a buffalo before and was not sure what to expect. However, to my surprise, the buffalo didn't react. It continued to walk slowly and eat grass. My friend walked nearby to keep me safe, and as we progressed together, I felt a bond and trust grow between the buffalo and me. After we returned to the farm, I gave the beautiful animal a huge hug and pat on the top of the head. It had been there for me and knew what I was going through on our long walk.

From that day forward, whenever I returned to the farm with my friend, I visited the buffalo and grew comfortable being close to that amazing animal. When I couldn't reach high enough to pick mangoes from a tree, I brought the buffalo under the tree so that I could stand on it to pick the fruit. This beautiful animal knew my real intention was never to hurt it, and I knew its intention wasn't to hurt me.

Looking back on those summer days spent on my friend's family farm, I feel grateful for the experiences and memories that were made. The hard work and dedication of the farmers, the beauty of nature, and the amazing animals, like the buffalo, left a lasting impression on me. I'm grateful for the bond and trust that grew between me and the buffalo, a magnificent animal that taught me a valuable lesson about overcoming fear and finding unexpected connections. To this day, I cherish those memories and hold them close to my heart, grateful for the lessons and joy they brought into my life.

12. The Joyful Sounds of Indian Wedding Brass Bands

It was a common practice in India for a wedding party to walk through the main streets of the village or city, shooting off fireworks and singing traditional wedding songs led by a popular marching band in colorful, shiny uniforms. The marching wedding brass band, with drums, flutes, and brass instruments, led villagers towards the amazing wedding ceremony while playing a mixture of traditional wedding songs and the latest Bollywood tunes.

I always enjoyed being in this music environment, so whenever I heard the wedding brass band's music playing, either in a village or city, my friends and I quickly ran to join the celebration. The band performed in an open area, so it was easy to see them playing their instruments and dancing. I watched them until the end of the wedding celebration, naturally curious about how the instruments worked. It was my desire and eagerness to learn, explore, discover, and figure things out. The whole experience intrigued me.

When the band members saw me following them for a while and observing them closely, they usually passed me a musical instrument I could play with my small hands. I would try to play along with them, and even though I wasn't very good, it was a thrilling experience to be part of the band for a moment. I felt a sense of belonging and pride when I was holding the instrument and playing it in front of my family and friends. It made me feel more connected to my culture and community.

Looking back on my experience of being a part of the wedding brass band, I realize how it made me feel free in the moment. It allowed me to explore my passion for music and discover new things, and to embrace my authentic nature. Through this experience, I came to better understand the traditions and culture of India and to appreciate the role that music and celebration played in bringing people together.

As I grew older and moved away from my hometown, I carried this lesson with me. I always sought out new experiences and opportunities to learn and grow in both my personal and professional life, even if it meant stepping outside of my comfort zone. It was this same sense of curiosity and eagerness that eventually led me to new places and new adventures, and ultimately shaped the person I'm today.

13. Discovering the Joys of Farm Life in India

Growing up, I wasn't fond of school or studying. Though I followed my teachers' instructions, I didn't invest as much time in preparing for exams as my classmates did. Even when I studied, my grades were generally lower than those of my friends. I often received poor grades and critical comments from teachers on my report cards, which left my parents disappointed. They had high hopes for my academic success, but I continuously let them down. Despite my promises to study more and improve my grades, I didn't have much interest in my studies.

Instead, I enjoyed spending time with my teachers and friends. I cherished the experiences of playing and engaging in playful pranks with my classmates, which made my school years in India fun and unforgettable. The end of the school year was always thrilling because it meant that the long summer vacation had arrived. I looked forward to this time because I could relax and enjoy myself without the pressure of schoolwork or exams. My parents sent me to my paternal grandparents' village, where I could spend time with my extended family, including cousins, uncles, and aunts.

Each year before my journey, my father took me on his bicycle to watch a children's movie at a nearby theater. After the movie, we ate dosa, at one of my favorite restaurants.

Dosa is a traditional South Indian dish, a thin, crispy pancake made with fermented batter, primarily consisting of rice and black lentils, and often stuffed with spiced potatoes. Then, my father rode me to the central bus station in the city of Vadodara in the state of Gujarat from where I could catch a bus to my paternal grandparents' village. The buses were affordable and comfortable, but they were also crowded and difficult to board.

As a quick and confident child, I often asked my father to lift me so I could get through the front seat's window opening and secure a seat by the bus drivers, thus avoiding the crowded entrance. I admired the drivers for their ability to operate the bus at high speeds and skillfully navigate through traffic and pedestrians.

When I arrived at my paternal grandparents' village, I walked to their home. In those days, we didn't have mobile phones or landlines, so my unexpected arrival surprised my grandparents and extended family. I was always welcomed with open arms and received so much love and affection from them.

My grandfather was an educated man who spoke three languages, including English. He was a traditionalist who enjoyed eating spicy homemade food and wore a white traditional hat with perfectly ironed white dhoti and kurta, both of which are traditional men's garments. Wherever he went, he carried a custom-made wooden cane with an elegant handle. He was a family man who was loyal to his friends and very caring with his grandchildren. He loved his agricultural and tobacco farming life and was passionate about it.

One of my fondest memories of my grandfather was our side-by-side walks on dark nights. He held a kerosene lamp as we managed the scheduled canal irrigation and treated the tobacco crops. Though he usually insisted I stay home and sleep, I never missed the opportunity to join him, even in the middle of the night. He shared stories with me about how to stay alert for any wild animals or bad people, and he showed me the sword inside the cane he always carried. We occasionally spotted coyotes, foxes, stray dogs, and deer, but we never had any close encounters with them.

Once we arrived at the farm, we spent several hours working on the tobacco plants under the dim light of the kerosene lamp. My grandfather showed me how to recognize the mature leaves, and how to handle and care for them. We then used a tractor and a trailer to transport the harvested tobacco leaves to the curing barns, where they were left to dry for several days before being packed and shipped to wholesalers.

These were some of my favorite memories from my childhood summers. I loved spending time with my grandfather, learning about farming, and being in nature. I also enjoyed spending time with my cousins and other family members, playing games and exploring the village.

Reflecting back, I realize that while I may not have been a strong student in school, I was learning and growing in other ways. I was learning about nature, farming, and life from my paternal grandfather, about family and community from my extended family, and about the joys of simple pleasures from my summer vacations. These experiences have stayed with me and helped shape the person I'm today.

14. Movies Adventure at Night in the Indian Village

During a summer night in my paternal grandparents' village in India, when I was a young child, I remember deciding to see a movie. Dressed in casual shorts, a colored T-shirt, and my usual slippers, I went next door to my cousins' home to see if they wanted to join me for a movie.

When they answered the door, before I could enter the home, I saw fear in the eyes of my cousins' uncle, who lived with them. He wouldn't let me speak to my cousins and mumbled, "All the kids are studying." He then turned and quietly told my cousins not to go with me to the movies and to study instead because I was on summer-break vacation in the village, and I didn't care about studying.

I felt sad and hurt, but I had come to know him and his personality well, and I didn't pay much attention to what he had to say about me. I knew who I was and wasn't there to prove anything to him. I just wanted to be a playful child and live in the moment. I didn't see the point of studying all day long when we were at the age when we should be playing and having fun. So, I ended up going to the movies alone and didn't miss out on the opportunity to experience something different in the village.

In those days, my grandparents didn't have a television in their home. Being a child, I enjoyed watching old Bollywood movies, so I went to a small place at the outskirts of the village where, using old VHS-VCR technology, movies were shown on a small twenty-inch television screen. The locals went there to watch a mix of old and newly released movies every night, and it was convenient for those who couldn't afford expensive movie tickets at the large-screen theater in the city. The building was concrete and had only one floor, with a pair of steel doors as its entrance. A man outside collected the cash-only entry fee. I paid fifty cents in Indian currency that my grandmother gave me. My grandfather assumed I was out playing with my cousins or friends and didn't know I was at the movie theater.

It was open seating, with mostly poor villagers in attendance; they sat on the tiny wood benches or the concrete floor, their backs against the wall, and their legs extended for comfort. A few people smoked their Indian-style tobacco cigarettes, and the ceiling fan spread the smoke, causing spirals to loom in the room. I sat on the bench next to guys with easily noticeable dark-red-stained teeth from chewing tobacco.

Returning to my paternal grandparents' home from the movie theater was the most difficult part of the night. The cool wind blew across the village, and I enjoyed the fresh air, but it was after midnight, and I was alone. The village was quiet, with only a few single-bulb light poles lighting the street. That late at night, the streets were empty, and all the homes had their doors and windows tightly closed. Villagers usually went to bed early and got up very early in the morning.

My grandparents' home was the last one in the gated cluster of eight homes. As I walked home, my mind couldn't help but dwell on the scary stories the villagers and my cousins had shared about ghosts living around my grandparents' gate. The area was scary, and everyone knew about the ghosts; each one had a name and its own peculiar demands.

To make matters worse, I couldn't shake the fear of the stray dogs that roamed the streets; they seemed to be stalking as they barked relentlessly at me, marking their territory and waiting to pounce. I stole a quick glance out of the corner of my eyes, and their glistening eyes and tongues signaled their readiness to attack. I kept my gaze fixed on my path, praying for someone to come by or open their windows, anything to give me the confidence to keep going.

I didn't want to run, for fear that it would only provoke the dogs and make things worse. So, I walked on, silently and determinedly, without making eye contact with the dogs. It took all my courage to keep moving forward, but I knew I had to keep going, no matter how terrifying the situation was.

As I approached our cluster residential area which was always closed at night with large doors. I began calling out my grandmother's name, or "Ba" as we call her, just as she had instructed me to do before leaving for the movies. She was going to open the heavy, tall wooden doors and large iron-chain door stopper that secured the area. Continuing to call out, "Ba, Ba, Ba," helped me stay focused and kept the negative thoughts of dogs and ghosts at bay. But when she didn't respond, my anxiety grew, and I began calling louder and faster, "Ba, Ba, Ba, open the doors!"

After waiting for a few more minutes, I realized I would have to go around to the back of the cluster of homes, through a dark alleyway, and try calling her from there. I knew it would be scary. But I was determined to go through with it.

Thankfully, as soon as I called her name from the back of our home, she heard me and replied, "I'm coming down to open the doors."

I breathed a sigh of relief as she opened the doors. Exhausted from my journey, I finally made it through the doors and stepped into the safety of my grandparents' home, where I immediately went to sleep next to my grandmother.

My grandfather was fast asleep in his own bed. During the humid summer months, we slept on the sheet-metal rooftops under the cool moon, enjoying the sight of the glittering stars above us. Some villagers used portable beds or comfortable sleeping bags, but I preferred the simple pleasure of lying beneath the open sky.

Feeling happy and securer there, I knew I was home and safe, sleeping next to my grandmother. These moments filled my heart with deep gratitude. Despite the risk of being yelled at by my grandfather, she offered me a bit of her savings for the movies. I always knew my Ba would wake up in the middle of the night to open the gated doors for me after the movie. It was our summer-vacation routine. The soft and peaceful light of the moon reflecting on my face was an amazing feeling, and it helped me drift off into a deep sleep.

15. Kite Festival: A Joyful Celebration in the Sky

The air was filled with excitement as the International Kite Festival, or Uttarayan, swept over the state of Gujarat, India. It was one of the grandest celebrations in the region, attracting millions of people of all ages. I was one of them, eagerly waiting for the festival to begin.

The Uttarayan, also known as Makar Sankranti, is a widely celebrated festival in India, marks the transition of the sun into the zodiac sign of Capricorn (Makar Rashi). One of the most significant aspects of Uttarayan in many parts of India, particularly in Gujarat, is the Kite Festival. It was originally a one-day festival on January 14, but it had evolved into a massive two-day event on January 14 and 15 every year. On these days, most businesses and schools were closed, allowing families to take part in the festivities.

The colorful kites, made from special paper and wooden sticks, were the stars of the show. Families spend weeks and even months preparing for the event, crafting or buying kites and string. The fun began on the rooftops, where friends, family, and neighbors gathered to enjoy the festive spirit, engage in good-natured rivalry, and partake in delicious Gujarati food and snacks, which are traditional to the people and culture of Gujarat, India, such as sesame seeds with jaggery.

The sound of Bollywood music filled the air, amplified by loudspeakers set up on the rooftops by various families. It was an exciting time for everyone, and I always loved being a part of it. While I lived in the city, I preferred to celebrate the Uttarayan festival in the village. There, the streets were less crowded, and the buildings were shorter, providing better views of the kites.

Up on the sheet-metal rooftops, the real fun began. Catching the loose kites passing by was more enjoyable to me than flying them. I competed with my cousins to see who could catch the most, moving from our rooftop to the connected ones of friends or extended family, depending on the direction of the wind. Running and jumping from sheet-metal rooftop to rooftop, we occasionally got stuck with roofing nails. It was always dangerous to run across the metal rooftops, as the chance of falling three to four stories to the ground was ever-present. The day was usually hot, and walking around without footwear was part of the fun. Wearing shoes would have made it harder to run and jump, increasing the risk of an accident on the rooftop.

Flying kites came with a price: bloody fingers. Most kite strings were coated with a special powdered-glass material, sharp enough to cut through the strings of competitors' kites. When trying to fly a kite, it was easy to cut my fingers. But the fun was worth it, and the pain was quickly forgotten.

On these days, they sell special finger tape to protect against cuts. But for me, the Uttarayan will always be a time of excitement, joy, and making memories that last a lifetime.

Section 2

Journey from Indian Village to the City Life

1. Journey from Village Life to the City

After I was born, my parents made the difficult decision to leave village life and move to the city of Vadodara, a vibrant and diversely populated city of Gujarat, India. In India, it's a common practice for a son, particularly the eldest son, whether married or unmarried, to live with his side of the family in a joint family and to take care of both his parents and family affairs. However, when a son, especially the eldest son, decides to move out on his own, it can be a difficult decision to break with tradition. This was the situation my parents faced when they decided to move to the city for a better life. My father had an older brother who could take over caring for my grandparents, but he and his family lived in a village far from the farm. It wasn't an easy decision, as it meant breaking with tradition by having a son and his family move out on their own instead of living in the joint family of the son's side. We had a large extended family in the village, and there were concerns that my parents wouldn't have the social, family, and financial support they needed in the city.

However, my parents had their own hopes and dreams, and they believed that village life would limit my experiences, education, and opportunities for independence and self-reliance. They wanted a better future for us and were willing to take the risk of moving to the city. My sister wasn't born yet.

My parents faced many challenges as they prepared to move. They needed a new job for my father that paid well, money for an apartment, food, and the basic expenses of city living, and knowledge of the right area of Vadodara in which to live, one with good schools for me.

During a job-finding trip to Vadodara, my father ran into one of his college friends who was sympathetic to his situation. His friend showed him an inexpensive, single-bedroom apartment with a small kitchen that was next to where he lived.

Although the apartment was still under construction and lacked power and running water, my parents were desperate for a place to stay, so they took it.

Living in a one-bedroom, incomplete apartment was challenging, but my parents were determined to make it work. My father and his friend took turns paying the monthly rent, groceries, and utilities. My father found a job at a bicycle stand that paid just enough to cover the basic expenses each month.

As time passed, my parents became more comfortable with city life, and my father started earning more money. This allowed us to move a couple of times until we found a decent environment and the perfect apartment.

Although the move was difficult, my parents' determination and hard work paid off. They were able to provide me and eventually my sister with a better future in the city, and I will always be grateful for the sacrifices they made to make it possible.

2. School Lunch in India: A Sense of Belonging

Every day of school in India was enjoyable for me. When I woke up each morning, I had a big smile on my face and was so excited to see my friends. I cared more about being with my friends than studying. I enthusiastically walked to school, most of the time alone. It was a long walk, about a mile, which was the normal routine for most children in India at the time. Like many of our neighbors, we didn't have the financial capacity to pay for private transportation back and forth from school, so I enjoyed my happy walk every day. Even if I could have, I wouldn't have replaced that walk with private transportation because it was just an amazing feeling, walking and wondering about all the people, shops, and street vendors I observed while passing by.

My school didn't have a cafeteria, so we brought food from home or ate from the street-cart vendors outside our school. We also were allowed to go to the nearby shops for spicy snacks, chips, cookies, or stuffed-potato pastries. There was a popular place within walking distance that made quick, hot Indian snacks to go. We had an hour-long lunch, so we had enough time to eat somewhere nearby and be back before the lunch break was over.

Most of my friends and I brought lunch provided by our loving mothers; it was fresh, home-cooked food made with love. My mother packed my lunch in a stainless steel container, which was tightly held together by clips on the sides. She made a diversity of delicious food dishes every day from scratch for our daily meals. She loved cooking and was serious about it. My most common lunch that I liked was homemade roti, which is a type of whole-wheat flatbread, along with sweet-mango pickles. Some of my friends occasionally brought lentil stew (dal), vegetable curry, roti, rice, fruit, yogurt with fruit, or juice.

When I ate at school, I ate with my friends, either on the ground in an open area of the school compound, or under a tree to protect ourselves from the hot sun. Sometimes we sat on top of the walls around the compound when our usual spots were taken by other students. My friends and I always shared what we brought for lunch. We offered one another our food and enjoyed eating together while talking, joking, and laughing.

Eating together helped us build better relationships, improved our social interactions, which, in turn, helped us do better in school. It was a harmonious feeling when we sat in a circle, shared food, and ate together. Mealtimes in India are traditionally the most important times for bonding with family, relatives, and friends; they are sit-down, social affairs.

Sometimes, I went home for lunch. We only had one hour, so I had to rush home and eat quickly the food my mother had prepared for me. She usually made my favorite Khichadi, which I would then add ghee to and enjoy with mango pickles. Khichadi is a traditional Indian dish made with boiled rice and lentils, known for its comforting qualities. Ghee is clarified butter made from butter, commonly used in

Indian cuisine for its rich flavor and aroma. After I finished eating, and then I quickly went back to school.

School ended at around 3:30 p.m. every day, and we walked back home, feeling happy and content after a long day of studying, playing, and eating together with other students. Once I got home, I played games, like cricket or hide-and-seek, with our friends in the playground near our apartment building.

Looking back, those were the best days of my life. I didn't have to worry about anything other than enjoying my time with my friends. I had the freedom to be myself, it was stress-free, and I enjoyed every moment of it. The experiences and memories from those days will stay with me forever.

3. The Umbrella Incident: Lessons and Friendship

The neighbors constantly complained to my mother about something I had done. I usually stood behind her or hid, feeling ashamed and embarrassed while neighbors complained. My mother just stood there and took all the complaints and insults, her face growing red with frustration and anger. Sometimes, when she thought I wasn't looking, I saw tears in her eyes. It broke my heart to see her like that, but I didn't know how to make things better.

It didn't matter to me that the neighbors complained; I wanted to be playful. My intent was never to hurt anyone, certainly not my friends. But sometimes small things happened, and the parents complained. We didn't have video games or mobile phones then. The types of games or things we had available to play with weren't always the best options.

One time, I unintentionally hurt my classmate, who happened to be one of my close friends. He lived in the compound next to where we lived. Our walking distance from school to home was the same. Sometimes I saw him walking alone, or he saw me, and we accompanied each other. We joked, laughed, and talked about homework, teachers, and friends. We also got into fights and arguments that ended up with my running after him, or vice versa.

One day, it was expected to rain, and we each had a small, child-sized umbrella our mothers had given us to carry to school. My mother, before giving me the umbrella, always looked in my eyes and with a straight face told me to be safe, careful, and not to play and hurt anyone with it. But umbrellas are convenient and useful playthings.

While walking home, clouds darkened the sky; there was lightning and very loud thunder. My friend and I started using our umbrellas as if we were two warriors fighting with swords. Every couple of blocks, we stopped and assumed the warrior's fighting position.

But, one time, our fake warrior fighting with swords continued longer than expected and got serious. While we were poking each other with our umbrellas, my friend grabbed the metal spike at the end of my umbrella while I still had ahold of the handle. Coincidentally, I jabbed my umbrella at him at the exact same time that he tried to jerk it out of my hand. As a result, he got poked in the corner of one eye. It was an unintentional act on both our parts; we were just having fun.

Once I got home, the clouds cleared, and sunshine came back. After a short time, my friend's mother and a group of his relatives came to our home to complain to my mother. They were saying harsh words to me outside our closed apartment door. My heart was pounding in my chest as I listened to their angry voices.

My mother didn't have a clue what had happened. Through a window by the door, she looked outside to see what was going on and, upon seeing who was gathered in front of our apartment, realized I must have done something. By this time, I was hiding in another room, feeling guilty and scared.

It seems that my friend's eye had started bleeding at the corner, and his family thought I had done it intentionally. So, they were angry. The complaining went on for a little bit, but then they calmed down when they realized that we were just playing around and that it truly was an accident. My mother apologized to them, and then once they left, she scolded me. I felt terrible about what I had done and promised her not to behave in such a way again.

My friend's eye injury healed after a few days, and we went back to being friends. But something had changed between us; we were both more cautious and hesitant in our play.

In the end, the umbrella accident taught me a valuable lesson about the importance of being mindful of others and the consequences of my actions. It also showed me the power of forgiveness and how it can mend even the most strained relationships. Although I haven't seen my friend in years, I still cherish the memories of our childhood friendship and the mishap that brought us closer together.

4. Overcoming Rejection and Finding Acceptance

Living in India during my childhood was a rewarding experience, but there were some moments that were challenging to manage. At times, there were quick answers and solutions that I could understand and apply, but there were also times that I found baffling. When faced with tough realities, I learned from those experiences. I found a way to adjust and not get stuck in the moment or form an opinion. I took the time to reflect.

It's part of my nature to be curious and to look for solutions with intense focus. I assert myself positively and visualize that better days are ahead, which helps me put aside the experiences and focus on what I need to do to keep moving forward. This tendency to approach challenges with a positive mindset and determination is an inherent part of my personality, rather than something I was taught during my childhood.

Later, many of these lessons and teachable moments formed the problem-solving foundation in my life that helped me through tough times in any scenario. They helped me learn more about myself, build tolerance, and endurance.

As I look back, there was one tough reality that I recall vividly. It had a huge impact on how I viewed my social interactions. I was school-age and at a very social stage of development; I was craving social interactions and trying to fit in with the neighborhood kids. Playing cooperative games was a big part of my plan; I wanted to make friends by doing things together with other kids. I was more attracted to other kids whom I perceived as similar to me. Fun, playful activities helped me figure out some ways to discover, identify, and share interests, or create things in common with my potential friends.

As I reflect back, I realize the importance of what I learned indeed came at a stage in my childhood when I was capable of learning, being creative, and acquiring numerous new skills and knowledge. Thus, I had an increased sense of awareness, belonging, and friendship with other kids in my age group. Playing cooperative games was a big part of my social interaction. I wanted to make friends by doing things with other kids.

I loved playing cricket, a bat-and-ball game played between small or large groups of players. It originated in England and dates back to the sixteenth century. Today, the game is played by millions in India and around the world, making it the most popular sport.

However, for me to play cricket, I had to find other kids who would play with me Exposing myself to my peer group of kids didn't come without risk. At first, I experienced negative reactions from them while trying to gain their acceptance. Rather than cutting off my contact immediately with these kids, I kept the lines of communication open and found compromises for each adverse situation. This helped me rekindle close friendships and connect with other kids. Instead of feeling rejected when the kids weren't being friendly, I used past teachable moments to motivate me to try harder to connect with them. It was a process that had a lasting impact; it has stayed with me throughout my adult life, influencing how I manage my personal, professional, and social relationships.

Eventually, after several attempts, the kids started to warm up to me. They started to acknowledge me, smile at me, and invite me to play with them. I was ecstatic. I had finally made some progress. It was the beginning of my friendship with that group of kids, and it opened up new possibilities for me.

From then on, after coming back from school in the late afternoon, I looked for my neighborhood friends to play street cricket. It was one of my after-school hobbies. My friends and I, though, were more interested in having fun and playing a casual game of cricket, than in creating a memorable experience. Anything with a hard, long, flat surface in the small streets, narrow lanes, or alleys covered with dirt, stones, tar, or concrete was good enough for us. We looked for a narrow street or an alley nearby where there were hardly any traffic or people on foot, on bicycles, or in vehicles. This gave us the open lane we needed to play cricket. It was always a lot of fun and an opportunity to connect with my friends. It was the only sport that I was really good at, at the time.

I became fascinated by the game as I watched adults play, and I learned about the offensive and defensive positions, as well as the winning strategies. As I got older, I sought opportunities to play with other kids in my age group.

One day, I visited the playground near our apartment, an open field where people of all ages could play cricket. From then on, every day after school, I went to the playground, where I found even more kids playing the game.

One perfect sunny morning over the weekend, I went to the playground. I saw some kids my age, whom I knew, playing cricket. I asked if I could play cricket with them. Some of them immediately replied no. I wasn't expecting a no from these kids I already knew. They told me to leave the playground because I was an outsider.

I paused and wondered how I could be considered an outsider when I was born in the same city as they were. However, we hadn't lived in the same neighborhood for very long, so maybe that was the reason. It wasn't a matter of caste, as we all belonged to the same caste and looked similar; rather, it was because we were newcomers to the area. I felt deeply hurt by these kids who resorted to name-calling, cursing at me, and treating me like an outsider. I felt rejected and uncomfortable.

However, the rejection didn't deter me from trying again to play cricket with the same group of kids. I figured that if I kept trying, they would eventually accept me, be friendly, and allow me to play with them. I didn't know of another place to play cricket, as most of the time people played near their homes. So, I had a better and easier chance of gaining acceptance with these kids than with a group of kids in another area.

Despite the painful and uncomfortable situation, I focused my attention on one mutual close friend in the group. It felt easier to gain acceptance by trying to convince him one-on-one rather than all of them at once. This close friend helped me get closer to this group of kids and move past the earlier rejection.

We would get together on weekends and play more games. We competed with other groups of kids from different areas for the winning prize: the cricket ball or the cricket bat. The ball and the bat weren't that costly, but for us, it was a lot, and we couldn't afford it. We were young and didn't have jobs. So, we asked our parents for some money to contribute to the prize. I was asked to pay more. Why? Because I was considered an outsider. If I didn't contribute more, I wouldn't be allowed to play. They bullied and cornered me into paying more than my share. This mistreatment left me feeling sad, disappointed, confused, and angry. All I wanted was to play cricket, be part of the team, experience the game, and have fun.

I felt powerless in the face of what seemed unfair. I then put aside our differences and focused on what I needed to do to be part of the team and play the game. I compromised, negotiated, and paid just a little bit more for my share of the prize so I could be part of the team. I realized that these kids had known each other for a long time and didn't know me as well. I saw this as an opportunity to grow my relationships with them.

After a while, I formed real friendships and bonded closely with all of them. We got together on the weekend and played more games. This helped us become better players both on offense and defense.

Over time, I became more confident and outgoing, and I made many more friends. I continued to play cricket and other sports, and I became quite good at them. But the most important thing was that I learned how to navigate social interactions, how to make friends, and how to be a good friend.

Today, I still carry these lessons with me. They have helped me to succeed in my personal and professional life, and they continue to guide me as I navigate the complex and ever-changing world around me.

Living in India during my childhood was a challenging but rewarding experience, and I'm grateful for all the lessons it taught me. As I look back on these cricket experiences, I realize that they taught me valuable lessons about perseverance, resilience, adaptability, and the importance of not giving up. They also taught me that rejection and exclusion are painful, but they can be overcome with patience and persistence. The moments of joy and connection with others taught me the value of friendship and the importance of building strong relationships.

Through it all, I learned the power of reflection and self-awareness. I learned to look at difficult situations not as obstacles, but as opportunities for growth and learning. Most importantly, I learned that no matter where life takes me, I have the skills and the strength to overcome any challenge.

My childhood in India was a time of wonder, adventure, and growth. It was a time that I will always cherish, and I'm grateful for the lessons learned.

5. Adventures on Two Wheels: Accident and Healing

On occasions, particularly during holidays, my family and I visited Kamati Baugh, one of the largest gardens in the city of Vadodara, Gujarat. To get there, we rode on my father's heavy-duty metal bicycle, which had large wheels, a straight bar across the front, and a solid stand in the back to carry a box, groceries, or even an additional person. This type of bicycle was commonly used in India to transport families of up to four people, provided that the rider was physically strong enough.

My father pedaled while I, still a child, sat in the front, holding on to the middle of the handlebars. My mother, dressed in traditional Indian sari, and my younger sister sat on the stand behind my father. My mother sat sideways with both feet on the left foot holder, holding my sister on her lap with one hand and my father's seat with the other. As we rode along, my parents chatted and created a pleasant atmosphere for our journey.

It took us well over an hour to reach the garden, and I could feel the wind and heat on my face, and hear my father breathing heavily as he pedaled. I didn't speak much during the ride, as I was too focused on the passing scenery, paying close attention to bicycles, speeding motorcycles, auto-rick-shaws, cars, buses, and trucks passing by.

To get to the garden, we had to cross a massive bridge, which was always a challenge for my father. The bridge was semicircular and peaked in the middle, making it the fastest and most convenient route to the garden. To carry us and the bicycle over the bridge, my father had to pedal as hard and fast as he could. Sometimes he could pedal all the way to the top with ease, but if a strong wind was blowing against us, we often had to stop near the top. Then, we all got off the bicycle and walked to the top of the bridge, where we got back on and continued our journey. Once we made it to the top, my father continued pedaling down the other side, which was much easier. Going down, we picked up speed, so my father carefully applied the brakes to ensure our safe descent.

To stay clear of fast-moving vehicles, my father always rode the bicycle on the curbside of the road. This meant we were far away from two-wheelers, three-wheelers, and four-wheelers. The side of the bridge was reserved for pedes-trians, and we stuck to the side to avoid any mishaps.

As soon as we arrived at the garden, my father secured the bicycle alongside others in the designated stand. We gath-ered our belongings, and my mother, who always brought snacks for us in her small handbag, paid for our entry into the garden. We started our visit by taking a leisurely stroll and then sought out a bicycle-rental stand for kids.

My parents always rented me a bicycle for an hour; my younger sister was too little for one at the time. As I didn't yet know how to ride a bicycle, my father assisted me by holding on to my seat as I pedaled slowly. However, after a few minutes, I invariably wanted to try it on my own. Though I'd inevitably fall and scratch my knees and elbows, it never deterred me from practicing and attempting to ride independently.

While my mother and sister relaxed on the lush lawn, enjoying the day and taking in the beauty of the trees, plants, birds, and the fresh aroma of the newly blossomed flowers, I practiced my bicycle-riding skills. Sometimes, we visited the planetarium or the small zoo that was part of the garden, adding more fun to our day out. Going to the garden became a way for our family to unwind and cherish our time together.

As I grew older, I became more confident in riding a bicycle, and I practiced with my father's bicycle at home. Even though it was too tall and heavy for me with a bar across, I persevered by holding on to the left handle with my left hand and the seat with my right hand, while putting my right leg across the bar to pedal, effectively bicycling with one hand. Though I fell a couple of times, I remained undeterred. Watching other kids ride their bikes made me aspire to become better. Whenever my father returned from work in the evening, I took his bicycle and practiced some more.

Soon, I gathered my friends on weekends or holidays when there was no school, and we planned bicycle races on a dirt road near our house. It brought us closer and gave us a sense of camaraderie. However, the group bicycle races didn't always go according to plan.

One time, we decided to make our bicycle races more challenging by setting up obstacles on our race path. We rode over humps, across potholes filled with rainwater, through forests, and over hills. These paths were much tougher than our usual rides, and all of the obstacles were natural. We didn't add anything to make it more difficult. We all agreed on the path to take, and we had someone at the starting and finish lines to monitor the race. There were no prizes—it was all for fun.

I was always competitive and wanted to win these bicycle races. However, unlike my friends, I didn't have my own bicycle that matched my height. We couldn't afford a new bicycle for me, so I used my father's. His bicycle was much taller and heavier than I was, which meant there was a greater chance of injury, especially since we didn't have any safety gear back then. I wore shorts, a short-sleeved shirt, and slippers since I didn't have any other casual shoes.

I pedaled standing up, giving it my all to win the race. I used every ounce of strength to push my father's heavy and oversized bike as hard as I could on the muddy path. Though I didn't always come in first place, I improved with each race. By the end, our clothes and bikes were caked in mud and dirt. We quickly washed ourselves and our bikes in a nearby pond or water tank, laughing and sharing stories about our rides, minor injuries, and close calls.

On one race day after days of heavy rain, we were more competitive than ever. We all wanted to do our best, pushing ourselves to go as fast as possible to achieve our best times. But disaster struck when I lost control of the bike while trying to navigate a slick hump of dirt. I fell hard on my back and cried from the sharp, intense pain shooting through my spine and down my leg.

My left shin was bleeding heavily, and my clothes were soaked with rain and mud. The bicycle had metal footrests attached to the front child's seat; they could be pulled out for use and pushed back in when not needed. It was the front edge of one of these metal footrests that had cut open my left shin when I fell.

My friends quickly noticed my fall and stopped the race to come to my aid. One of them fetched water for me, while the others looked for a way to stop the bleeding. They found some large leaves from the nearby forest and tied them together to fashion a makeshift bandage for my wound. One friend tore his shirt and applied firm pressure on my leg to staunch the bleeding. We all sat there for a while until the bleeding subsided.

We were all apprehensive that my parents would be angry, not just with me, but with all of us, and that they might even tell my friends' parents what happened. They all knew each other since we lived in the same neighborhood; it was a tight-knit community. We agreed that we would keep quiet about the incident and let my wound heal over the next few days. It was normal for us to have some bruises and scratches from playing, as we often wore shorts and didn't have proper footwear.

However, we faced a big problem—my father's bicycle was damaged beyond repair; the handlebars and wheel rims were bent. It was the only bicycle in our family, and my father used it for work. He had recently purchased it, and it had cost us a lot of money. In those days, bicycles were an investment for many families; they lasted for years and were bought from hard-earned savings. I was really worried about telling my parents about my wound and the damaged bicycle. I was scared of how they would react.

After my bleeding stopped, my friends and I walked together with our bicycles. They helped me get to my home and then left to return to their own. I brought the damaged bicycle inside and left it where my father always parked it in the first-floor lobby; we lived in a second-floor apartment. I locked the bicycle and quickly went to sleep.

The pain in and around my wound was intense, and I just wanted to rest. My mother and one of my maternal aunts were busy in the kitchen, and my father was outside at a social gathering with his friends. My sister was playing outside with her friends. So, no one had noticed anything out of the ordinary yet. I woke up from a deep sleep to the sound of loud voices. My mother and aunt were crying and asking me what happened. They had noticed a large puddle of blood at the side of my bed. I told my mother about the accident, and she immediately asked our neighbor to fetch my father from where he was. In those days, we didn't have mobile phones.

When my father arrived home and saw the state of our bicycle, he was furious. He demanded to know what happened, and despite my intense pain and nervousness, I knew I had to confess. Through tears, I gathered the courage to explain what occurred. My parents were understandably upset.

Since my father couldn't use the bicycle, he carried me in his arms to our neighborhood family doctor's office, which was within walking distance of our apartment. The doctor made me his priority after seeing the seriousness of my injury.

When the doctor opened the wound that my friends had covered, he found a deep cut that required stitches. The doctor joked to keep me calm while he cleaned and sanitized the wound. His assistant prepared what the doctor needed to stitch me up with a long needle. I was scared when I saw the needle, but my father held me down on one side, while the doctor's assistant held me tightly on the other, as the doctor stitched up the wound on my left shin and covered it with medication, cotton, and a bandage.

Once it was over, I felt better and was ready to go home. We continued to follow up with the doctor for a few weeks until the wound was fully healed. After the accident, I became more cautious when it came to riding bicycles and participating in physical activities.

This experience taught me the importance of friendship, cooperation, and communication. My friends stayed with me and supported me, even though they themselves were scared of the consequences from their parents. Our friendships grew stronger. We played fun games and engaged in outdoor activities, but we didn't race bicycles after the accident. I learned from the consequences and didn't repeat it.

As time passed, my interest in bicycling faded away, and I turned my attention to other hobbies and interests. However, the memory of that accident has stayed with me, and I often think back to that day and wonder how my life might have been different if I had never gotten on that bicycle. Despite the injury and pain, I'm grateful for that experience, as it taught me valuable lessons about the importance of safety, the fragility of life, and the kindness of friends. I still have the scar from the injury; it reminds me of this childhood incident.

6. Indian Market: Lessons in the Art of Persuasion

Growing up, I often visited the local vegetable and fruit markets in India with my mother or other relatives. These bustling markets were a hub of activity, filled with vendors hawking their wares and shoppers haggling for the best prices, as vendors used their salesmanship skills to entice clients to buy. These trips are some of my fondest childhood memories, and they taught me important lessons about the art of persuasion and successful negotiation. In this story, I will share one particularly memorable experience from those market visits.

On a scorching summer day in Vadodara, the sun beat down mercilessly as bright-white clouds drifted through the deep-blue sky, breaking apart and reforming in a stunning display. Like many of our neighbors, my family didn't have a refrigerator at the time, which meant we couldn't buy fresh produce and keep it for long. Instead, it was a daily ritual to visit the local fruit and vegetable markets and pick out what we needed for that day's meals.

In addition to the local fresh vegetable and fruit markets, there were vegetable and fruit vendors who roamed the streets on four-wheeled wooden carts, making it incredibly convenient for stay-at-home mothers with young children and elderly people who couldn't walk well. This stress-free experience allowed people to buy what they needed right in front of their homes, without having to go on a long ride using private or local transportation or getting stuck in traffic.

Street-cart vendors offered a diverse range of small goods, including plastic and stainless steel containers, snacks, cookies, bread, cold drinks, ice cream, and quickly prepared food. Some vendors even roamed the neighborhood on foot with large bags filled with brand-new traditional and modern clothing for men, women, and children, as well as kitchenware, women's accessories, and other small items, like organic vegetable oil, honey, soap, and shampoo. These products were available for purchase at low prices and could be conveniently bought on the purchaser's front porch. Whether returning home by car, motorcycle, bus, or on foot after a long day's work or after exhaustive exams, people could easily pick up last-minute items they needed from these vendors.

As I reflect back on those mobile-cart vendors today, I realize that their concept was and still is a brilliant and innovative one that can be found in India today. It's particularly beneficial for stay-at-home mothers and the elderly, who can conveniently purchase goods without leaving their homes. This concept is reminiscent of the current trend of online grocery ordering and home delivery, which has gained immense popularity in recent times.

Visiting the fresh vegetable and fruit market with my mother was an unforgettable experience. The area surrounding the market was bustling with energy and life—the sounds of people chattering, the crowds jostling for space, the traffic, and the vividly colored, freshly grown vegetables, such as tomatoes, carrots, potatoes, onions, ginger, green peppers, lemons, eggplant, okra, dill, cucumbers, green beans, bottle gourds, cabbage, and cauliflower. The market also offered various types of herbs, each with its unique and fresh aroma, such as mint and cilantro. And the fresh fruits, with their mouthwatering, sweet, and natural flavors, and vibrant hues were just as tantalizing, including bananas, papayas, guavas, oranges, apples, pineapples, grapes, berries, watermelons, other melons, and seasonal mangoes.

The vendors at the fresh vegetable and fruit market comprised men and women of all ages, many of whom had inherited this family tradition that dates back several generations. For them, it wasn't just a livelihood, but a skill, a job, and a family-owned business that they knew by heart. They took great pride and comfort in being vendors and worked very hard for long hours, often laboring intensely, either individually or as a group with their family members, such as married couples, parents, children, siblings, or friends. Some even brought their young children along to play while they sold vegetables and fruits from a mobile cart, stall, or off the ground. The work was physically, mentally, and emotionally exhausting, and some days were harder than others. They ate when they got a chance, or skipped meals if they were too busy selling, grabbing a quick snack or a cup of chai when time permitted. Despite the challenges, these vendors remained committed to their work; they took immense pride in their family traditions.

The vendors' ability to attract buyers and market their products was truly impressive. Their knowledge, insights, and wisdom about selling, marketing, and persuading buyers all came from practical, real-life experience. They had remarkable personalities and skills that had been honed over the years. They made direct eye contact with a smile, were always polite, and called over everyone, from children to the elderly, with proper gestures and manners. They knew their products inside and out and could immediately tell you about a product's contraindications, benefits, origin, and how it differed from those sold by other vendors nearby. They communicated well, clearly, and simply, avoiding conflict and exuding confidence in their goods. Even when their sales were minimal for the day, they maintained a positive attitude and remained their authentic selves. It was truly a testament to their dedication and passion for their work.

The vendors worked tirelessly, calling out and competing for the attention of potential buyers. There were no pricing labels; they negotiated to make a penny's profit, all while keeping their loyal clients happy and coming back. They had a long-term vision and didn't force anyone to buy. They were well-versed in the prices of every other street vendor in the entire market, and they made informed decisions to set their prices competitively. Despite interacting with hundreds, if not thousands, of buyers every day and week, they took the time to learn the names, family history, and friendship connections of their regular clients. They were mobile, patient, and decisive, always ready to move on to the next potential sale. Their commitment and hard work were truly admirable.

Indeed, the experiences and skills gained from interacting with street vendors in local markets can be invaluable in various aspects of life. The ability to tell a compelling story, provide excellent customer service, and build authentic relationships with others are crucial in any professional career or business. The vendors' knowledge of their products, competitive pricing, and negotiation skills can also be applied in many different settings. Their adaptability and decisiveness in meeting clients' needs can be valuable in any leadership role.

As I reflect back on my experiences at the local vegetable and fruit markets in India, I realize that the skills I learned there have had a lasting impact on my life and have helped me in many aspects of my personal and professional development. Later in my career, as I worked with Japanese clients, I found that these same skills were essential in building better relationships and achieving successful outcomes in negotiations and contract agreements. My experiences in Japan reinforced the value of the lessons I learned at the market, and they continue to guide me in my work today. The ability to communicate effectively, build authentic relationships, and understanding the needs of others is truly invaluable in any professional context.

Section 3

Pursuit for a Better Future: Navigating the American Dream

1. A Family's Pursuit for a Better Future: India to America

Traveling by train in India is a unique and special experience that I cherished during my childhood. Trains offer a smoother ride than buses and are a convenient and affordable way to explore the spectacular, diverse natural landscape of India. This is especially true for long overnight journeys; the sleeper cabins offer truly relaxing travel.

On a warm summer night in the early 1980s, I stood outside the main entrance of the Vadodara railway station in the state of Gujarat, India, with my parents and relatives, waiting for my maternal grandmother and aunt. The station was crowded with passengers from all walks of life. Some were waiting in long queues to purchase their tickets, while others were already waiting for their trains to arrive. Some passengers were sitting on the floor inside the station, while others sat on the steps of the train station's entrance. Some were standing, while others sat on their luggage or heavy boxes. Parents were saying goodbye to their children, and some were smoking or reading the newspaper.

My grandmother and aunt were permanently moving to the United States of America. My grandmother's brother, who was living in the United States, had sponsored them for legal entry into the United States, based on their blood relationship, in order to build a better future for the family. It was a proud moment for our family to see the courage of my grandmother and aunt as they traveled on their own to a totally unknown country, to a new culture and lifestyle, without a lot of knowledge about the country and with very little money. They didn't even speak English.

My grandfather and father were going with them to Mumbai, a bustling city located on the western coast of India, where the International Airport was situated, to assist them and drop them off. They had booked an overnight sleeper cabin on the train for a relaxing journey. It was a momentous occasion for our family as they were the first ones to leave India and move to the United States.

Many relatives and friends came to the train station to say goodbye and receive blessings from my grandmother. Most of them immediately bowed down and touched the feet of my grandmother, an age-old custom of showing respect to our elders and asking for their blessings. Amidst the emotional farewells to my grandmother and aunt, some came with happy faces, and others with tears in their eyes and sad faces, but all showed great affection and love. Some brought with them hand-tied, fresh, and colorful flower garlands as a gesture of respect and honor. When the garlands became too heavy for their necks, my grandmother and aunt put some on me, much to my delight.

As we made our way towards the departure platform, the vibrant energy of the station enveloped us. The bustling scene of people waiting for their trains created a buzz of excitement, and the various food and drink stalls added to the lively atmosphere. The aroma of freshly made chai, hot samosas, fried pakora, chana dal chaat, masala loaded vada pav, and spicy snacks filled the air, tempting our taste buds. Vendors both inside and outside the train sold cold drinks, ice cream, flavored milk, soft drinks, and freshly made hot chai. We walked past stalls selling colorful scarves, bangles, and other traditional Indian accessories, all of which added to the sensory overload. The vendors were shouting out their wares, hoping to catch the attention of passing travelers. Announcements in different languages blared over the loudspeakers, announcing the arrivals and departures of trains. The constant chatter, laughter, and commotion made the train station seem as if it were a small city. The station, with its blend of colors, sounds, and flavors, was a true reflection of India's vibrant and diverse culture.

My grandfather and father had seats reserved in the same cabin. Suddenly, reality kicked in when I saw my mother and relatives in tears and deeply emotional. They were bowing down to touch the feet of my grandmother to receive her final blessings. My mother was especially emotional because she was the oldest daughter in the family and had a very deep, loving, and close relationship with my grandparents since she was a child. She, no doubt, was feeling the additional responsibility on her shoulders to look after and take care of her father, brother, and four sisters who were young, single, and staying in India. Though my mother was married, it was part of her nature to take care of and look after her siblings and parents.

When I saw other children board the train, something inside of me clicked. I wanted to go too. As a child, I had never been on a long overnight train ride. I was also emotional about seeing my grandmother and my aunt leave.

I was close to them, and they had showered me with so much love. So, I asked my mother if I could go with them. She said no, but I tried to convince her that I would behave well and that I would be back with my grandfather and father in the next few days. She again immediately replied no and reminded me that I didn't have a ticket.

While the adults were having their conversations, my cousins and I quickly boarded the train just to look around before it departed. There were leather sleeper seats and people getting into them, making themselves comfortable for the long ride. It was a special feeling to be on the train. I really wanted to ride on this train, to spend time with my grandparents, and to feel the experience of train travel.

Since my mother had already said no twice, I decided to ask both my grandparents if I could go with them to Mumbai; I promised to behave well. They resisted at first, but I was persistent, and they knew I wasn't going to give up. Finally, they decided to take me with them to Mumbai and paid for my half-priced child's train ticket. My mother had some extra clothes for me that were passed on to my father. I was full of joy and excitement.

Soon, it was time for the train to depart, and family and friends waved goodbye to my grandmother and aunt through the iron-barred open window. The guard blew the whistle and waved the green flag, and as the train began to move, a loud air horn sounded the warning. The wheels slowly turned on the railroad track, and there were several distinct sounds, including the locomotive-engine noises as the train left the station. On the platform, families and friends waved their hands to say their final goodbyes with tears in their eyes.

The train started to move faster to reach its average speed. The engine had a dual capacity, allowing the train to harness electrical power in urban areas or use diesel in more remote areas of India. As the train picked up speed, I watched the world go by outside the window. At night, I could see city lights, lights in homes and on vehicles. My grandparents had brought along some snacks, and we ate as we rode.

When it was time to sleep, we adjusted the seats to sleep; a convenient option for overnight travel, it consisted of six beds that could also be converted into seats. The cabins had small windows for natural light and ventilation. My grandfather helped me climb up to my bed, which was shared by other family members. I was nervous at first, but once I got in, I realized how comfortable it was. I could hear the sound of the train and feel the gentle rocking motion. We heard the soulful voices of singers traveling from station to station, performing devotional songs, qawwalis, or Bollywood songs, and collecting money in exchange, which lulled me to sleep. It was an unforgettable experience.

In the early morning hours, we arrived at Mumbai's central railway station, a large, old building designed as a major stop for local, intercity, and express trains. It had many platforms that were well-connected by a bridge walkway extending between adjacent platforms with their associated stairs. The station was bustling with people, not just from our train, but from other trains that had arrived earlier or were scheduled to depart later. The noise and chaos of the station were overwhelming, with the sounds of train whistles, vendors hawking their wares, and people rushing to catch their trains.

My father found the famous porters, who were paid laborers dressed in red uniforms with gold metal badges on their left arms. They carried the suitcases and handbags of traveling passengers on their carts, on their heads, and in their hands. They were always in high demand because they knew exactly all the train numbers and travel destinations, where to go, which platforms to board from, and where to find your coach number and your seat. They carried our suitcases across the platform to the taxi stand, where we caught a cab to the home of my grandmother's brother who lived in Mumbai.

The next night, we accompanied my grandmother and aunt to the Mumbai International Airport for their flight to the United States. My aunt was very emotional as we arrived at the departure gate, and she faced the reality of leaving behind her family, friends, and the only country she had ever known to venture into the unknown world of the United States of America. She knew that she would be facing many challenges as a woman with limited knowledge of the language, culture, and customs in a foreign land. However, my grandmother and aunt both possessed natural leadership qualities, which enabled them to understand that their sacrifice was temporary, and that they were paving the way for a better future for our family.

My grandmother never hesitated, nor did she question how life in America would be. She always had a deep faith and an optimistic view, believing that they would find a way to overcome any obstacles that came their way. With this positive attitude, they left for America, filled with hope and dreams of great possibilities.

Their journey to America was a defining moment in my life; it taught me the importance of family, resilience, sacrifices, and the courage to pursue one's dreams. It showed me that, no matter how challenging life may seem, there is always hope. Witnessing their courage in pursuing their dreams, despite the challenges they faced, taught me that anything is possible with hard work and determination. As they embarked on a new chapter of their lives, I felt a mix of sadness and pride. I will always cherish the example my grandmother and aunt set for me, and their journey will continue to inspire me throughout my life.

In the end, my train journey with my family taught me more than just how to travel comfortably through India. It showed me the value of adventure, independence, and family, and it gave me a newfound appreciation for the beauty of our natural world. As my grandmother and aunt departed for America, I felt a sense of hope that anything is possible if we are willing to take risks and step outside of our comfort zones. Life is full of opportunities, and we must seize them, even if they require taking risks and stepping outside our comfort zones. Although farewells can be difficult, the love and support of family will always be with us, guiding us through the challenges of life's journeys. As I look back on that train ride, I'm grateful for the memories and lessons it provided, and I'm reminded that every journey, no matter how long or short, has the power to transform us in unexpected ways.

Looking back on my grandmother and aunt's journey, I'm filled with gratitude for the memories and lessons it provided. It was through their efforts, determination, hard work, and sacrifices that the way was paved for our better future as a family in the United States. As I continue on my own journey through life, I will always carry with me their love and memories.

2. Hope and Resilience: An Indian American Family's Story

Upon their arrival in the United States of America (USA), my grandmother and aunt temporarily stayed with the family of my grandmother's brother, who had sponsored their entry into the country. Her brother recognized the potential for opportunities in the United States and believed that his efforts would provide better prospects for their family. During this time, the Indian American community in the United States was still very small, with few Indian grocery stores, restaurants, places of worship, or organizations available to assist my grandmother and aunt with the American way of life.

Some of the challenges they faced included finding appropriate clothing, as my grandmother had never worn Western clothes, like pants and shirts, in India, but had to wear them for work in the United States. As soon as she came home from work or outside, she changed back into her traditional Indian sari. My grandmother used to go to the temple daily, as she was so devout, but when they moved to the United States, there weren't many temples she could attend. Both my grandmother and aunt were vegetarians, but in the United States, they couldn't find many vegetarian-food vendors or restaurants in those days. They had to rely mostly on home-cooked food. They didn't have many friends, so they made friends at work or at occasional Indian-community events.

In addition to these challenges, my grandmother and aunt didn't fully understand the American culture and its systems, such as banking and employment, so they relied on others in the community to help them navigate these processes. Theyalso struggled with language barriers, speaking broken English and learning as time passed. They didn't have enough money saved to have everything they wanted in their apartment and had to prioritize their expenses. Indian groceries, such as rice, vegetable oil, roti flour, dal, and spices, weren't readily available near their home; they had to drive for over an hour to purchase them.

Despite the difficulties they faced, my grandmother and aunt persevered, learning to adapt and overcome each challenge they encountered. Driven by their determination to create a better life for themselves and our family, their unwavering dedication eventually paid off. As they gradually assimilated into the American culture and values, they found success through hard work. Their story is a remarkable example of personal victory, great achievement, and overcoming adversity in a foreign land as Indian Americans. Through their hard work and perseverance, they eventually sponsored other family members, like my grandfather, aunts, uncle, and us to enter the United States. Their experience is a powerful testament to their strength, resilience, determination, and the human spirit in overcoming obstacles and achieving success in the face of adversity.

3. Starting from Scratch: Building a Life in America

In the late 1980s, my family—my parents, my younger sister, and I—left India and came to the United States in search of a better future. As was true with the earlier wave of Indian immigrants, we arrived with little of material value.

I still remember the mixed emotions I had about leaving India. On one hand, I was excited about the United States and its opportunities, but on the other hand, I didn't want to leave my childhood friends behind. The thought of not seeing them again was difficult to bear.

My paternal grandparents, who lived in a small village in Gujarat, India, were an important part of my life. I couldn't imagine growing up without their love and support. Their wisdom and stories of hope and faith had inspired me through difficult times.

We left all of our belongings behind, storing some things and giving away others to our relatives and my parents' friends. We only brought personal items with us, such as pictures, important documents, and my parents' wedding album. We didn't have many possessions in India, and we didn't have to worry about leaving behind valuable items, like a car or motorcycle.

On the day of our flight to the United States, my parents had only eighty dollars in their pockets. They spent fifteen dollars on food and beverages during a long layover in London, England. Customs at the airport in the United States charged us a fifty-dollar fine for prohibited food found in our suitcases, leaving us with only fifteen dollars when we arrived. Upon our arrival, my maternal uncle and grandparents greeted us warmly at the airport, lifting our spirits after a challenging and long journey.

Two days after we arrived, my uncle took my parents shopping for Western clothes to wear at work, such as sweaters, pants, and shirts. It was a new experience for my mother, who had never worn Western clothes before. She felt shy and embarrassed at first, but knew it was necessary to assimilate into American culture, especially at work. My mother also found it awkward to wear pants and shirts instead of saris, the traditional Indian garment, but she eventually got used to it.

Finding jobs wasn't easy for my parents. They didn't speak English, and they had no car to help them adjust to American life. They also faced other challenges, such as not finding vegetarian options at local restaurants and living a frugal lifestyle. We had to shop for Indian groceries every week or two, which was difficult as the nearest store was over an hour away. After finally finding jobs, my parents worked long hours and weekends at two jobs. My sister and I also faced obstacles in the new school system and unfamiliar environment. These are just a few of the hardships we endured. However, we faced these challenges together as a family and grew stronger through our shared experiences.

Despite the difficulties, my family persevered, learning to adapt and overcome each challenge we encountered. Driven by our determination to create a better life for ourselves and our family, our unwavering dedication eventually paid off. As we gradually assimilated into the American culture and values, we found success through education and hard work.

4. Starting Over in America: A New Home in a New Land

When we first came to the United States, we didn't have much of material value. We temporarily stayed at my maternal uncle's apartment; he had just gotten married, and his wife and my grandparents also lived with us. My parents, who had some education and spoke little English, knew they needed to find jobs quickly to become independent. They applied to various factories in the area with the help of my uncle. Eventually, both of them landed manufacturing jobs that required more physical labor than speaking.

My father worked at a chemical factory, which proved to be difficult due to the hazardous chemicals he handled. He came home with his clothes and boots stained and damaged from the chemicals, his hands covered in chemical residue. However, he persevered and worked hard to provide for us.

After three months in the United States, we finally moved into our own apartment. It was a small space, barely big enough for our family of four. But it was ours. My parents had worked tirelessly, taking on manual jobs and earning only the minimum wage, just to pay for our daily needs and monthly expenses. They scraped together every penny to cover the rent, electricity, phone, groceries, and school supplies for my sister and me.

Our grandfather, who had come to the United States a few years before us, helped us in any way he could. He paid for our first month's Indian groceries, which my parents accepted with gratitude. But, soon after, they returned the money to him. They were determined to provide for us, to give us a better life than we had in our homeland. It was an overwhelming challenge, but their determination and perseverance never wavered.

Our apartment had only one bedroom; a two-bedroom apartment was out of our financial reach. At first, we didn't have any furniture, but over time, we received some used furniture from relatives, including a dining table, chairs, a mattress for my parents, and a sofa. For almost eight years, we lived in that apartment. My parents slept on a used mattress, while my sister and I used sleeping bags on the carpeted floor. We made the best of what we had, but we never forgot our dream of one day having a better home. After eight years, we finally moved to our own two-story home, which was a significant improvement for our family.

My sister was the only one who spoke English fluently because she had attended a private English elementary school in India. She helped translate for us and answered anonymous phone calls we received at the apartment.

One of the main challenges we faced as a family was not owning a car. In America, owning a car was an essential part of daily life, and this was especially true in the smaller cities and suburbs where we lived. Most forms of public transportation, like buses and subways, were not available, making it difficult to get around. Even though my parents had never driven before in India, they knew they had to learn if they wanted to be independent.

My parents relied on paid carpools with coworkers to get to work, while my uncle taught my father to drive on the weekends. It took many weeks of practice, but eventually my father passed both the written and driving tests at the local state testing facility to receive his first official driver's license. My mother followed suit soon after. However, when my parents finally saved enough money to buy their first used car for around two thousand dollars, it turned out to be a bad decision. The car constantly stalled and overheated, and it required both feet to drive, even though it had an automatic transmission. After spending a lot of money fixing it up, we only kept the car for a year before we were able to buy our first brand-new car.

As children, my sister and I understood the value of hard work and sacrifice. We didn't ask for anything special or complain about our situation. We knew our parents were doing everything they could to provide for us, and we respected them for their unwavering dedication. We saw them working long hours, day in and day out, even on the weekends; they took on extra jobs and sacrificed their own needs to ensure that we had everything we needed. It wasn't easy, but we did the best with what we had. We learned to appreciate the small things in life, such as having a roof over our heads and food on the table.

For most of those years, we didn't have much in the way of home entertainment. Cable TV and video games were luxuries we couldn't afford, and the internet wasn't even available at the time. Instead, we had to make do with what we had. I still remember the day I found that small black-and-white TV in the garbage area outside our apartment building. Only one channel worked on it, and the reception was terrible. We had to move the TV around the apartment window to find a clear signal, and sometimes I even had to tie a thin wire from the television antenna to the apartment's aluminum window screen to get better reception. But it was better than nothing, and it gave us a small escape from the hardships of our daily lives.

Despite the countless obstacles and hardships we faced, my parents never gave up on their dream of building a better life in America for our family. They were determined to provide us with a brighter future, even if it meant enduring a difficult and challenging journey. Along the way, we encountered many struggles and setbacks, but our family remained united, always supporting each other with love and a shared commitment to succeed.

Over time, my sister and I have become more fully aware of how much our parents truly sacrificed just to provide us with a better life. We see how they gave up their own dreams to ensure that we had the opportunity to pursue ours.

Today, our family is doing well. My sister and I have successful careers. We have achieved the American dream that our parents envisioned for us. But we have not forgotten our roots. We still remember the hardships we faced, and we remain grateful for the lessons we learned along the way. We learned the value of hard work, sacrifice, and perseverance.

5. Harsh Realities of My Life in High School

On a warm and charming fall morning in the United States, I had just finished a breakfast of cereal and milk. My maternal uncle appeared, from his bedroom, in the kitchen, where we were staying temporarily at his apartment, and asked if I was ready for school. Being excited to see the American school system for the first time, I eagerly agreed, although I was still recovering from jet lag and adjusting to the change in weather from India.

However, I was also nervous about my first day in an American school. The school year had already started in August, and students were usually enrolled months in advance. Due to our late arrival in the country, I was starting school late, a few weeks after the high school year had already begun.

I dressed in a long-sleeved shirt, blue jeans, and comfortable shoes and joined my uncle in his burgundy-colored classic Oldsmobile car to drive to the high school in our district. The school was impressive from the outside, with a large building and clear-glass windows. The hallways were filled with students wearing casual clothes, laughing, talking, and teasing, and I couldn't help but wonder if any of these strangers would become my friends someday.

After arriving, we made our way to the Admissions office on the second floor, where my uncle explained our purpose. The secretary contacted the student counselor responsible for new-student enrollment, who assigned me appropriate classes for a first-year freshman. She provided me with a printed copy of the class schedule for the semester and the standard high school curriculum, which contained all the required classes to graduate high school in four years.

Though the curriculum contained a long list of classes, my priority was English. As a non-native speaker, I had to learn to read, write, and understand English to pass any courses, much less graduate high school. The counselor assigned me to English-as-a-Second-Language (ESL) classes to satisfy the English requirements for high school graduation. We agreed that if I exceeded expectations, I would move to higher-level English classes each semester. The class schedule was designed to offer each student the opportunity to explore their interests, acquire new skills, and take charge of their own study habits, allowing them to develop good relationships, gain knowledge, have diverse experiences, and ultimately graduate with good grades.

The following day, I started school as a freshman, and my uncle showed me the school bus stop, which was located just around the corner from our apartment. Every morning, I was to catch the school bus there and be dropped off again in the afternoon.

The next morning, I woke up feeling nervous but determined to make the best of my first day at school. I ate my usual breakfast, got ready, and grabbed my new book bag, which contained a simple notebook, a pencil, and school documents. As I waited at the school bus stop with other students dressed in casual clothes, I couldn't help but feel out of place. When the bus arrived, I hesitantly stepped on board, unsure where to sit.

As I nervously scanned the bus for an open spot, a student in the front caught my eye, and I sat down next to him. He turned to me and stared, making me feel even more uncomfortable. The bus was full of diverse students of different races and ethnicities. The bus driver kept glancing at me through the mirror above him, likely noticing that I was a new student. I felt self-conscious and either kept my head down or looked away.

Once we arrived at the school, I was lost and confused, not knowing where to go. As I stood at the entrance, feeling overwhelmed and alone, a kind woman approached me and tried to help. But I couldn't understand her questions in English and had to show her my school documents. She then took me to the student counselor's office.

The counselor recognized me from the day before and helped me with my class schedule and where I needed to go for each class. She kindly explained the process of moving from classroom to classroom, which was different from what I was used to in India. She called someone to take me first to the office where they issued student IDs and then to my first class.

The math teacher in my first class looked intimidating, with a long wooden ruler in his hand and a stern expression on his face. He didn't speak kindly to me, but he did help me find an open desk at which to sit. All day, I struggled to understand the lessons and what was being said in English. I felt alone and overwhelmed.

During lunch, I had no food or money and sat alone, feeling lonely and doubting why I was even in school. Walking around the hallways, I saw students talking openly and fluently in English, which amazed me. I felt as if I didn't belong.

As the day went on, I went from classroom to classroom, trying to find where I needed to be next. I got lost multiple times and had to ask for help. But, even then, I struggled to communicate and understand. Finally, at the end of the day, I boarded the school bus, feeling relieved that it was over.

It was a difficult and painful experience. Despite the challenges, though, I persevered and worked hard to adapt to my new environment. It wasn't easy, but I learned to navigate the school, make friends, and eventually feel as if I belonged. Everything progressed as well as could be expected until, a few months later, we moved to a new apartment.

On my first bus ride to school from our new apartment at the affordable-housing complex, things were different. As the last student to get on the bus, I couldn't find an open seat near the front and was told to go to the back. But as I moved towards the middle of the bus, I was met with insults and offensive remarks directed towards my Indian heritage. The students called me names, like "Dot," and told me to go back to my country.

I didn't understand all the words, curse words, and phrases they used, but I could tell from the tone of the words that they were racist in nature, unkind, and uncalled for. So, I kept my mouth shut and ignored them. But that didn't work well. These students became more aggressive in their bad behavior. They pushed me around more as I came down the aisle and directly to my face called me some nasty names with intensity. When I tried to pass by their seats, they put their feet across the aisle, trying to block me or trip me by making me fall over their feet while I wasn't looking down. But I stayed quiet and found the courage to continue moving to a safer seat in the back of the bus, even when there were plenty of open seats available in the front and middle. Most of the students had the entire bench seat to themselves, but they weren't going to allow anyone who looked like me to sit next to them.

This drama continued not just on the bus ride from our apartment to school, but also on the return. I was pushed around, punched, and called names. The sad reality was I was bullied by White students and Black students bigger than I was, and not just the boys. A few of the girls also got involved or supported the boys. I wasn't the only one; there were other students, mostly of Indian origin, who were also bullied and pushed around.

We couldn't complain to the bus driver because none of us spoke fluent English. As new immigrants, we didn't know to whom we should be complaining. Neither did we think the bullying would stop by complaining; it would probably make the situation worse. The bullies often followed us after we got off the bus, walking aggressively beside us, insulting us, and even throwing things at us to get our attention. We feared confronting them because we knew we would have to face them at our apartment complex after school.

I thought that if I stayed silent, they would stop. I was too small physically, compared to those strong kids, so getting punched in the face or anywhere on my body was extremely painful, and I bruised easily. When I was beaten, I hid the bruises from the teachers and students, even from my parents. I was totally defenseless and helpless as I didn't have the physical strength and support of any other students on the bus to stand up or fight back. Some of those kids were double my size. I grew angry, frustrated, and often cried over this mistreatment.

My only safeguard was to sit next to other students who had come from India or Asia, sit with girls who were nice and polite, or sit in an empty seat, if available, in the very back of the bus. Sometimes, when things got really difficult, I stayed after school and took a later bus in the late afternoon, which was mostly for students who stayed after school for activities or sports. The after-school bus had a lot fewer students, and the mean kids weren't on that bus, which helped me avoid more conflict. But that also meant I had to stay after school for a couple of hours, so I wandered around the school or spent time at the library, studying or doing my homework.

Not only were the bus rides difficult, but I also experienced bullying, name calling, and pushing both in class and while going from class to class. Often a group of students looked for me and followed me from my locker to my class. When they saw me walking alone down a long, empty hallway, or in the stairway between floors, this group of students came over, took my books, and ran away, or knocked my books out of my hands.

The bullying didn't end during my four years of high school. However, it got much better when, with the support of my student friends, I stood up to those boys. We knew that direct confrontation wouldn't make the bullying stop, but we had to show confidence in ourselves by standing strong together. We became courageous and inspired to stand up for ourselves. That really helped reduce bullying among the people of Indian origin in our high school during the time I was there.

Looking back, I realize that the bullying I experienced wasn't my fault. It wasn't because I was different or because I had done something wrong. It was because some students had prejudices and weren't mature enough to respect and appreciate diversity. It's not easy to be different in a new country, especially when you are trying to adjust to a new language, culture, and environment. But I learned that it's possible to overcome adversity by finding strength in oneself and building relationships with others who share similar experiences.

Now, as an adult, I'm grateful for the experiences I had in high school. They taught me resilience, empathy, and the importance of standing up for what is right. I hope that my story can inspire others who may be going through similar challenges to stay strong, seek support, and believe in themselves.

6. My Place on the Sidelines: High School Physical Education

In physical education class, the teacher issued me and the other students an attendance number. That number corresponded to numbers stamped on the gym floor. We were given only five to ten minutes at the beginning of class to change into our gym clothes in the locker rooms and get to our assigned attendance number in the gym so that the teacher could take attendance before the class started. I always changed quickly and was one of the first in the gym, dressed in comfortable shorts, shirt, and gym shoes, ready and eagerly awaiting the chance to play.

Once attendance was taken, the teacher usually had a couple of students, both boys and girls, take turns choosing players one by one to form their own teams. Unfortunately, I was overlooked by my classmates who saw me as unathletic and a person unaware of the game rules, despite my eagerness to learn and participate. As a result, I never had the chance to develop my skills in dribbling, hitting, catching, throwing, or sending the ball over the net, nor did I get a chance to understand the rules of the games.

Day after day, for almost the entire school year, despite my eagerness and readiness to play, I was never given the chance. I was inevitably left standing alone, leaning with my back against the closed retractable gym bleachers…again and again…watching from the sidelines as my classmates ran, jumped, and competed, leaving me feeling invisible and left behind…wishing I could join them. It was painful; I felt sad and hopeless, rejected and so embarrassed, and downright pathetic.

It felt even worse that not even the physical education teacher cared that I was by myself on the sideline, simply waiting anxiously, hoping for a chance to be just like the other kids, to play with the other kids. It was hard to believe that I was now being judged based on my inability to keep up with the rules and techniques of unfamiliar sports. These difficult, enduring moments often took me back to my glory days in India when I was considered one of the most athletic among my peers.

After nearly one and a half years of attentively observing the games that my peers played, I picked up the basic rules of the games. As I became more familiar with the high school system and improved my English communication skills, I no longer felt the need to force myself onto teams that didn't want me or looked down on me. Instead, I decided to play on the sidelines by myself or with people who looked like me. My challenge was finding an open court to play with my own ball, as most of the courts in the gymnasium were occupied by our class and other physical education classes.

To find a group of students to play with, I looked around for friendly students, students who had arrived in the country recently, or students from my ESL class. Some of these students I had already bonded with, so I asked them to form a team with me so that we could play together, however little we knew about the game. When we had enough people for a small team, then it was easier to ask for our own court and balls. This also helped us to get attention from the teachers who came over to explain the rules or show us how to play as a team. We didn't play hard and fast, like the other students and teams in the class, but we had fun playing together and learned the game in the process.

Over time, the students on my team came to me right away when the class started. I grew into a friendly and natural leader for them, and they began to look up to me. They started taking their own initiative to challenge themselves to learn to play well, stay active, and have fun together, regardless of how little they knew about the sport.

This process allowed me to become a team player and fostered strong friendships among us. We created lasting bonds and memories, and when the time came to pick a team, we formed our own team quickly, just as the other students formed theirs. We were ready to face the competition within the physical education class.

Throughout the school year, we played a wide variety of sports, including individual sports, like wrestling, gymnastics, and badminton, to team sports, like volleyball, football, soccer, and baseball. The team sports were usually co-ed, both boys and girls playing together. As I learned more about the different sports, the more I made it my responsibility to share my knowledge with my new friends, who might not have had the chance to play otherwise, I remained patient, persistent, and determined to teach them how to play the games to the best of our ability despite setbacks, teasing, and frustration.

And it paid off. Eventually, I became a natural leader for my team, and my friends began to look up to me. We played hard, but we also played fair, and we learned so much from each other. The games we played helped me improve my cardio, jumping ability, strength, flexibility, balance, and coordination.

Looking back on those difficult days, I can't help but feel a sense of sadness and frustration. But I also feel proud of myself for not giving up, for persevering even when things were tough. And most of all, I feel grateful for the amazing friends I made along the way and for the memories we created together.

7. The Challenge of Speaking: Math Class Helped Me Find My Voice

Math class was always my biggest challenge, not because of the numbers, but because of the language. English was my second language, and every time I sat in that classroom, surrounded by native speakers, I felt as if I were drowning. But, one day, I found the courage to stand up to my fears, and it changed everything.

In my math class, I found myself grappling with more than just equations and formulas. I was grappling with my fears, my doubts, and my insecurities in front of a class full of native English speakers. It was a daunting experience that left me feeling small and uncertain.

Mr. Scott, my math teacher, paced the room with his long wooden ruler, announcing the day's lesson. I sat in my seat, my head down, hoping that I would blend in and not draw any attention to myself. But as fate would have it, Mr. Scott called out my name, along with seven others, to come up to the front of the class and write out the solutions to the homework problems from the previous night's assignment.

My heart sank as I realized that I was the only one in the class who wasn't a native English speaker. I could feel the weight of everyone's eyes on me as I hesitantly made my way to the front of the classroom. As the other students confidently began writing out their solutions, I felt frozen, my mind racing with thoughts of inadequacy and self-doubt. What if I made a mistake? What if I couldn't explain my thought process? What if they laughed at me?

I stood there, my hands shaking as I held the chalk, and tried to speak. But the words wouldn't come out right. My broken English and thick accent made it difficult for me to communicate effectively. The other students looked at me with a mix of confusion and impatience, and I could feel the tears welling up in my eyes.

It was at this moment that Mr. Scott stepped in. He recognized my struggles and refused to let me give up. He urged me to keep trying, to write out my solution and explain it to the class, no matter how hard it seemed. With his guidance and support, I was able to finish the problem and present my solution to the class.

But I couldn't shake the feeling of embarrassment and inadequacy that lingered long after that day in math class. The classroom, which once felt as if it were a safe haven, now seemed daunting and intimidating. Every time Mr. Scott called on me to explain my homework, my heart raced, and my hands shook uncontrollably. The fear of making a mistake or stumbling over my words consumed me. I began to doubt my abilities and questioned whether I belonged in that classroom.

The other students didn't seem to understand the depth of my struggle. They spoke English fluently and were able to explain their homework with ease and without a second thought. I felt like an outsider, as if I didn't belong. I didn't have the luxury of speaking English fluently, and it felt like an insurmountable barrier that held me back from truly succeeding in school.

It wasn't until Mr. Scott pulled me aside after class one day that I realized he saw something in me that I couldn't see in myself. He told me how proud he was of my progress and encouraged me to keep pushing myself. His words gave me the motivation to persevere.

Mr. Scott never gave up on me. He pushed me to keep trying, to keep standing up in front of the class and explaining my work. His encouragement and support helped me to slowly gain confidence in myself and my abilities. And as time passed, I began to realize that I wasn't alone in my struggle. There were other students in the class who also faced their own fears and obstacles, and we were all in this together. Eventually, the once-intimidating classroom began to feel as if it was a place where I could belong.

Despite my initial doubts and fears, I came to realize that I was capable of succeeding in this class, regardless of my language barriers. With Mr. Scott's unwavering encouragement and support, I was able to find the courage to overcome my fears and become a confident student. By the end of the semester, I had even grown to love math, a subject I once thought was out of my reach.

In the end, I learned that courage isn't about being fearless. It's about facing your fears head-on, even when it's terrifying. And with the help of Mr. Scott and my classmates, I was able to overcome my fear of public speaking and learn to embrace the challenges that came my way. The classroom that once seemed daunting and intimidating became a place of growth and learning, a place where I could truly thrive.

8. My High School Adventure: Finding My Passions

High school can be a challenging time for anyone, but for me, it was even more difficult as a non-native speaker of English. As a newly immigrated individual to the United States, I found it difficult to adjust to both the new environment and the American school system. However, my last two years of high school as a junior and senior proved to be a time of immense personal growth. I became more confident in my abilities, both mentally and physically. This was aided significantly by the fact that my English-language skills had improved significantly, as compared to my earlier years in high school. I also had gained a deeper understanding of the high school system in the United States, which allowed me to navigate it with more ease. Furthermore, I had improved my relationships with both students and teachers and had learned how to handle challenging situations with greater resilience. I had become more comfortable reporting any incidents of bullying or personal attacks to my teachers or the dean's office, which helped create a safer and more supportive learning environment for everyone.

During my final two years of high school, I discovered a passion for celebrating cultural diversity and promoting awareness among my fellow students. Working alongside my English-as-a-Second-Language (ESL) teachers, we established the first-ever International Student Club. As a proud founder and member, I helped plan and organize various events throughout the year, including the celebrations of Independence Day and New Year's Day from different countries. These events were joyous celebrations of diverse cultures; we displayed traditional clothing and souvenirs and even hosted special music events and lunches from different cultures. The club was a wonderful opportunity to educate and promote awareness of different cultures, and I was honored to be a part of it.

During this time, I discovered American football and quickly fell in love with the game. I studied the rules, positions, and techniques in my gym classes, and worked hard to improve my strength and speed. My goal was to make the high school football team as a wide receiver. I worked hard to improve my skills and physical strength, spending long hours in weight-lifting sessions and running on the track. I studied the rules and positions of the game, and became more knowledgeable and confident with each practice.

However, my dreams of playing football came to a sudden halt when my parents expressed concerns about the serious physical injuries associated with the sport. While it was a difficult decision to let go of my aspirations, I knew that my safety and well-being were the top priority. With the encouragement of my family and friends, I turned my attention to safer sports that still allowed me to showcase my athleticism.

After trying out for baseball and tennis, I discovered a real passion for soccer. I earned a spot on the fifteen-player boys' soccer team and spent the next two summers dedicated to the sport. The intense training and long practices under our coach's guidance were challenging, but ultimately rewarding. Despite the academic demands of my high school courses, I found a way to balance my commitment to the team with my studies. As the soccer season kicked off, I was filled with a sense of pride and excitement about representing my school on the field.

As I look back on my high school years, one of my most cherished memories was the time I spent on the boys' soccer team during my last two years of school. We competed in both home and away games, and the spirit of competition was intense. The support we received from fellow students was truly heartwarming, and their cheers fueled our passion to perform our very best on the field. From the rigorous training to the long practices and summer workouts, my teammates and I pushed ourselves to the limit to prepare for each match. But it wasn't just the games themselves that made the experience so rewarding; it was the camaraderie that developed amongst the team members.

Looking back on my high school years, I realize that the challenges I faced and the obstacles I overcame helped me gain the skills and knowledge that have stayed with me to this day. With the support of my teachers, friends, and family, I was able to become more confident, more involved, and more aware of the world around me. From the International Student Club to playing on the boys' soccer team, I learned the importance of diversity, teamwork, and dedication. These experiences not only enriched my high school experience, but also prepared me for the future.

9. Reflection on High School: Remarkable Teachers

High school is a time of growth and change, and for me, the teachers I had along the way were instrumental in shaping who I'm today. My high school teachers were some of the most inspiring and impactful individuals in my life. In particular, my biology teacher had a heart of gold, bringing milk and cookies to class and treating us as if we were her own children. Her kindness and warmth made class a joy to attend.

My chemistry teacher, on the other hand, was a true master of his subject. He always dressed sharply in a tie and dress pants, and wielded a wooden measuring stick with ease as he pointed out the periodic table on the wall. While he may have lost his cool when my lab partner and I caused a bit of chaos, we always respected and admired him.

I also had some amazing math teachers during my high school years, not the least of which was Mr. Scott. They challenged me to think critically and approach problems from different angles, which helped me develop a strong foundation in math. But it wasn't just their teaching style that left an impact on me—they also showed genuine caring for their students and their students' successes.

My English-as-a-Second-Language (ESL) teachers were instrumental in helping me improve my English skills, and they gave their all to make sure I was able to communicate effectively. One English teacher even encouraged me to join the school's golf team, which was coached by him.

Meanwhile, my physical education teacher was a big supporter of my dream to play on the football team, even if he couldn't directly help me.

In woodshop and electrical classes, my teachers helped me unleash my creativity and challenged me to push my limits. I fondly remember my geography teacher who spent extra time with me after school teaching me how to read maps, which came in handy when my family took our first long road trip.

Finally, my driver's education teacher was a patient and compassionate instructor who was always there to help me improve my skills. Despite his occasional outbursts when I made mistakes, he truly cared for his students and even let me drive home a few times when I missed the bus. His kindness and support helped me build confidence in my driving abilities.

Looking back on my high school years, I'm filled with immense gratitude for the incredible teachers who played such a significant role in my life. They all made me a better person and set me on the path to success.

My high school years were a transformative time in my life, a journey filled with challenges, growth, and meaningful connections. Though the beginning was tough, as I adjusted to my first experience with the American school system, I tapped into my resilience and grit with the support of remarkable teachers and classmates. The valuable lessons I learned, the precious memories I made, and the lasting relationships I formed during that time have shaped the person I'm today. My high school years were truly remarkable and unforgettable, and I will forever hold them dear to my heart.

10. Forging My Own Path: Success in Higher Education

My journey towards a university degree was filled with obstacles and challenges, from financial struggles to the pressure of succeeding. But with perseverance and a strong support system, I was able to push through and emerge stronger on the other side.

After graduating from high school, I enrolled in community college for two years. Without any mentors to guide me through my college decisions, I sought advice from my trusted friends on their plans for college. Most of my friends had chosen community college as an affordable and practical option, which was preferred by our families who couldn't afford expensive universities. So, I, too, applied to the local community college in my county.

At that time, a traditional college or university experience wasn't suitable for me. I was undecided on what I wanted to study and needed a more affordable option. My parents worked long hours and made minimum wage, so finding an affordable college close to our home was my top priority. College education in the United States is costly; tuition and fees, commuting, dorms or apartments, meals, and other personal expenses can easily accumulate to more than what most people make in a year. Many students in such situations turn to student loans, but I didn't want to amass debt before obtaining a college degree and a high-paying job.

In hindsight, given my circumstances, choosing to attend community college was one of the best decisions I could have made. Community college provided an affordable path towards a real university experience in the United States. While attending, I had incredible experiences with fellow students, acquired new skills, and worked on group projects. It was the perfect forum to gain the essential tools necessary for my higher-education journey.

After attending community college for two years, I transferred to a four-year university in my state as a third-year bachelor's degree candidate. Most of the course credits I earned at the community college transferred to the university and fulfilled its basic requirements. Even after spending two years at community college, I had not yet decided what to study for my bachelor's degree. I had a variety of interests in medicine, pharmaceuticals, accounting, and engineering, but I found more interest in technical courses and ultimately chose to pursue electrical engineering as my undergraduate degree. This decision was based on a long-term vision of job security and better pay.

However, money was still a challenge for my family. Some of my parents' savings went toward paying for my university tuition each year. To help with expenses, I found work during winter and summer breaks and saved money. I worked part-time at my university's pavilion as an usher during basketball games or large events, like concerts. I directed people to their seats, kept a watch out for trouble, and cleaned the floor after the game or event was over. The extra money I earned covered my personal expenses, such as buying clothes or going out to eat with my friends. I was deeply grateful for my parents' support and assistance in paying for my university tuition and expenses, and I wanted to do everything I could to find part-time jobs while studying to ease their burden.

Enrolling in university means different things to different people. Some attend for a degree, others as the natural progression of their lives, while still others may do so to fulfill their parents' expectations. For me, a combination of these reasons motivated me to enroll in university. What I observed during my time there was that having good professors and supportive friends and family were key to making the most of the experience. My professors challenged me to do better, while my friends rooted for me and provided a source of understanding and inspiration.

11. My Journey to Landing a Job: From Rejections to Success

Finding a job is a journey that tests our resolve and our patience. In my own experience, I faced numerous setbacks and challenges, but ultimately emerged stronger and more determined than ever before.

As graduation approached, the pressure of finding a job weighed heavily on me. I knew that the first step was to prepare for job interviews, but without a mentor, the process was daunting. I spent countless hours reading books and consulting friends who had been through the process before. In those days, there was no internet to help with research and interview preparation, so I practiced asking myself different questions that a recruiter might pose. I did this silently or in front of a mirror in my dorm room until I had the confidence to convince a recruiter that I had the character, confidence, knowledge, and skills to excel at the job.

I took advantage of the mock interviews offered by the college Career Center, but the feedback was brutal. I knew that I needed to improve my interview skills, but I felt overwhelmed by the pressure to showcase my abilities and personality in the span of a few minutes. They advised me to focus on being positive and motivated, but that was easier said than done.

When I received an invitation for an on-campus interview with one of the top consulting companies just weeks before graduation, I was over the moon. I didn't have any business attire, so I went shopping for my first suit and tie. I spent days researching the company's background, history, and services. But the night before the interview, I was consumed with anxiety. I couldn't sleep, and I was worried about the questions that would be asked by the recruiter. Despite my nerves, I tried to remain positive and motivated.

The next morning, heart pounding, I arrived at the Career Center for the on-campus interview. As soon as they called my name, a familiar voice caught my attention. It was one of my college friends who had graduated a year or two before me. At first, I thought it was a good omen to have someone I knew on the other side of the table. But as I followed him to the interview room, he started asking me questions. It soon became apparent that he wasn't interested in my abilities, my hard work, or my achievements. Instead, he was using the interview as an opportunity to talk about himself and his own travels. I was surprised.

My first job interview was a disappointing experience, but I tried to learn from it and move forward. I took a few days' break and returned to the Career Center to look for another job. Despite setbacks and frustration, I was determined to find a job and refused to give up on my goal. Every day, I remained focused and persistent, never losing sight of the ultimate goal. The process was difficult, and my self-doubt grew with every passing day, but I never let my spirit diminish. I continued to push forward, even in the face of adversity.

As time passed, it was disheartening to see my friends landing jobs while I was still struggling. I felt guilty and ashamed for not having secured a job immediately after graduation. The waiting game was taking a toll on my mental and emotional well-being, and my parents were understandably concerned about my job status. I scoured the job postings in the local newspaper and visited the university's Career Center multiple times, hoping for a breakthrough.

Finally, I received a ray of hope when my maternal uncle reached out to me with a job opportunity at his company as a telecommunications engineer. I felt renewed hope and sent in my resume.

A few days later, I received a call for an interview. I prepared thoroughly and answered questions confidently, remaining positive and focused. After I met with different senior members of the engineering team who were working on a project for a Japanese company, I left feeling optimistic, but deep down I wasn't sure if I would actually land the job.

Finally, after weeks of anxious anticipation, I received the long-awaited offer letter. Tears of joy streamed down my face as I read the words. The company was offering me a position and the opportunity to work on a large project for a prominent Japanese client! Despite the salary being lower than the market rate, I was overjoyed and accepted the offer without a second thought.

It had been a long and arduous journey, with multiple rejections and moments of self-doubt, but I had emerged stronger and more resilient. The struggles I faced during my job search taught me the value of perseverance, determination, and patience. Before starting my new job, I took a trip to visit my paternal grandparents in India. I felt a deep sense of gratitude for the support of my family and friends who had encouraged me every step of the way.

Section 4

Cultural Crossroads in Japan: Connections, Work, and Celebration

1. My Business Trip to Tokyo: A Cultural Awakening

One sunny spring day, a long black limousine arrived outside my house to take me on a journey I had never expected. I was about to embark on an international flight to Tokyo, Japan, as part of a new project for my company. Dressed in a dark suit, the limousine driver came to the door and loaded my luggage and laptop bag into the trunk.

As I prepared to leave, my mother brought me a small bowl of yogurt and a piece of jaggery, a family tradition to bring good luck on a journey. Seeking my parents' blessings, I touched their feet before they walked me to the car. They marveled at the luxurious interior, took pictures, and admired the designer lights and leather seats.

As I was about to step into the limousine, my mother gave me a tight hug and whispered her final blessings, telling me to take care. I felt her heartbeat against my chest and her tears of joy against my face. I knew how proud she was of me and how far we had come after years of struggle. With a heart full of emotions and determination, I got in the limousine and set off on a journey that would change my life forever.

My first business trip to Tokyo, Japan, was a cultural awakening that immersed me in the world of new cultures, traditions, people, food, languages, and experiences that would forever shape my perspective on international business.

During this trip, I was leading a large telecommunications engineering project for one of the largest telecommunications Japanese companies in the world, known for its innovative services and advanced technology. The success of this project was crucial to our company, and I felt a tremendous responsibility to ensure its success.

From the moment I stepped off the plane at Tokyo Narita International Airport, I was transported to a world of new experiences. Everything was so clean and organized, and the airport signs were perfectly placed, making it easy to navigate. After booking the airport bus to my hotel and paying in Japanese yen, I proceeded to the bus stop outside the exit gates. The people handling my ride were professional and polite, setting the tone for the rest of my trip.

We were on our way to Makuhari, a bustling business district just outside central Tokyo, located along the scenic shores of Tokyo Bay in Chiba Prefecture. The area is home to a mix of global corporations housed in modern, towering skyscrapers, as well as shopping centers, restaurants, and other commercial establishments.

My hotel, a tall brown building with large windows, was a luxurious twenty-four-floor representing a top Japanese hotel brand, with a real treat for the senses. The lobby was impressive and spacious, with high ceilings and a sleek, modern design, while its towering height added to the overall grandeur of the building. As I checked in, I noticed the smooth marble counter under my fingertips, and the fragrance of fresh flowers. The staff were attentive and intent on providing excellent service; they were polite, professional, and helpful. I felt truly welcomed. My hotel room was comfortable, its decor was traditional Japanese, and it had all the modern amenities. Sliding windows opened to a stunning view of the city skyline and Tokyo Bay.

Although I was tired, hungry, and jet-lagged, I felt the urge to explore the area. My work was to start the next morning in one of the client's buildings in the business district. I didn't know how far I had to go or how to get there from the hotel, so I decided to do a dry run while it was still daylight. That way, I could learn the city's layout and time my route, ensuring that I would be on time for my first meeting. I wanted to make a good impression on my Japanese colleagues and our client.

The hotel's concierge was incredibly helpful, providing me with local maps and advising me to walk to the client's office instead of taking a taxi. I walked along the clean streets of Makuhari, Tokyo, enjoying the fresh air and the pleasant scent of the city. The well-designed streets were equipped with traffic signals and walkways, making navigation easy. I leisurely walked for fifteen minutes from my hotel to the client's office building, admiring its modern rectangular design. The building, which was a research and development center, was a stunning glass building with dark-tinted windows. It was the tallest building in the area and offered magnificent views of the surroundings.

As I approached the building, the open area leading to the entrance invited me to explore further. The building was in the bustling business district, surrounded by other global companies, like Fujitsu, IBM, and Sharp Electronics, as well as the AEON Tower, the largest exhibition hall in Tokyo, and other amenities, such as banks, convenience stores, food courts, and restaurants. The train station was also in close proximity. The area was vibrant and dynamic; the city's retail district was only a short distance away.

As the sun set, I returned to my hotel, feeling grateful for the opportunity to experience such a lively area and the Japanese culture. The excitement of the new adventure ahead filled me with anticipation.

2. Navigating the Cross-Cultural Workplace in Japan

The next morning, as I walked towards the client's building, my emotions were a mix of excitement and nervousness over leading a large telecommunications engineering project for one of the largest Japanese telecommunications companies in the world. The success of this project was crucial for our company, and I felt immense pressure to ensure its success. However, I was also filled with gratitude for the opportunity to work on my first project in Japan. I reminded myself to stay calm and confident as I entered the building.

A large, two-way glass sliding door automatically opened, revealing a stunning view of the lobby. The spacious lobby had a relaxing Japanese ambiance that immediately put me at ease. The shiny white-stone flooring and warm lighting created a welcoming atmosphere. The large, tall, clear windows gave the traditional Japanese decor a contemporary look; this blend was part of the overall design of the building. A large reception and waiting area with a couple of large sofas welcomed visitors. For those waiting, there was also a small lounge in the corner; it appeared to offer traditional tea and coffee. In the center of this vast space, a large television played news programs.

Walking into the building, a mix of excitement and nervousness washed over me. Everywhere I looked, I saw well-mannered Japanese men and women dressed like top management executives. It was hard not to feel intimidated by their presence.

As I watched others in the lobby, I noticed some bowing to each other as a sign of respect, which was a cultural learning experience for me. I later learned that Japanese businesses are highly formal, and their employees place great importance on appearance. The receptionists, all dressed in matching company dresses, greeted me with polite bows. I was asked for my name and the reason for my visit. I presented my bilingual business card in Japanese, and she promptly informed one of my colleagues that I had checked in.

The receptionist issued me a company badge and kindly escorted me to the elevator. She informed me of the floor I needed to be on and assured me that someone would be waiting for me. While waiting, I noticed various services offered in the building, including dining facilities and convenience stores. This showcased the company's focus on creating a functional and comfortable working space. I felt confident that this was a company that valued not only business success, but also the well-being of its employees.

Stepping into the elevator, which had clear-glass walls, I observed its ultrahigh speed and quietness. Prerecorded announcements in Japanese were delivered in a soothing voice as the elevator stopped at different floors. People in the elevator stood quietly, their eyes fixed on the large display showing the floor numbers.

Once I stepped out of the elevator, I was warmly greeted by one of my colleagues who then escorted me to the client's office area. The office space served a dual purpose as both an office and a system testing center, complete with duplicate telecommunications networking systems found in commercial sites. I was uncertain about what to expect. As we approached the area, I took deep breaths to manage my nerves. This was the moment I had been waiting for all my life. I had worked hard in college and at work, preparing and planning for this project and this trip. I realized how fortunate I was to have the opportunity to work on my first project in Japan. With a renewed sense of purpose, I committed to taking full responsibility and doing everything in my ability to ensure the success of the project across key stakeholders and cross-functional teams.

Prior to entering the office and systems testing area for the first time, my colleague instructed me to remove my shoes and wear a pair of spare slippers that were provided. The soft fabric of the slippers kept my feet warm and comfortable. Later, I learned that this was a long-standing Japanese tradition in some offices, restaurants, and homes to maintain cleanliness and prevent the spread of dirt. I wanted to follow these cultural customs and show respect for local traditions while working in Japan.

Natural light poured in through large windows on the left side of the office area. Tall buildings surrounding ours were visible, creating a mini downtown atmosphere. The right side was used as office space; it was equipped with computer systems but lacked personal office space and private meeting areas. There were no partitions, cubicles, or individual office phones. The entire office design highlighted the corporate emphasis on transparency and accessibility.

I found an open desk among my colleagues and quickly set up my workspace, embracing the collaborative nature of the office. Once settled in, my Japanese colleague briefed me on the agenda and the structure of our project kickoff meeting. As I looked around the open room, I felt a strong sense of shared purpose and camaraderie. The lack of personal space made it easier to connect, communicate, and collaborate with my colleagues and the client's team. I was eager to see what we could achieve together.

Although I wasn't very knowledgeable about Japan, my colleagues in the United States had prepared me well for the Japanese way of life and work. They provided me with technical and cultural information, including the proper exchange of business cards, to help me interact effectively with my client and local colleagues. My colleagues also warned me that the client's management team was one of the most demanding and well-organized, and that I had to communicate carefully in meetings because their management wouldn't hesitate to have me replaced if they didn't approve of me. Deep down, I felt anxious and fearful of failing and letting down my colleagues and company, but I saw this cross-cultural work environment in Japan as a valuable opportunity to learn and grow. Adapting quickly was important to my success.

3. Managing Pressure: My First Project Meeting in Japan

As the client's team arrived, we began our first project kickoff meeting in a spacious, modern conference room with large windows overlooking Tokyo Bay, which provided a stunning view of the Makuhari skyline. The room was equipped with state-of-the-art audio and visual systems, and at the center of the room was a sleek, long table. The meeting consisted of members from our in-country management, sales, and engineering teams, as well as senior managers and engineers from the client's side. While I recognized a few faces from the client's side from our previous interactions in the United States, I was hesitant to reach out and make a connection, as I wanted to stay focused on the official meeting agenda. I didn't want to divert attention from the official meeting agenda as we sat on the opposite side of the table, next to my English-Japanese interpreter and local colleagues. The seniority on the client's side was reflected in their seating arrangement, with the highest senior manager in the middle and the lower-ranking managers on either side, as is the Japanese custom. I knew that a productive kickoff meeting was important for the success of the project.

The meeting began with a well-respected, high-level senior manager from the client's team giving an introduction and welcoming statement, followed by self-introductions from all participants. As I looked around the room, I was struck by the presence of these amazing and successful Japanese professionals. Just before it was my turn to speak, I felt nervous about addressing the group, especially since most of them didn't speak English fluently. To ensure that I conveyed my message effectively, I quickly jotted down key points I wanted to address. When my moment came, I felt all the attention, anticipation, and eyes looking at me. However, I immediately realized that I was speaking too fast and using long sentences because of my nerves. The Japanese-English interpreter from the client's side was struggling to keep up with me, which made it challenging to communicate effectively. Nevertheless, as the meeting progressed and we exchanged questions and concerns, we eventually found a rhythm that worked for us.

The client's project manager then went through the meeting agenda, discussing the project's purpose, goals, deliverables, tracking issues, and each team member's roles and responsibilities. Key success factors, expectations, communication plans, and project plans were laid out, and reports were given on the project's daily progress, escalation paths, and working hours.

Although the client didn't state it explicitly, it was clear that I needed to demonstrate my ability to work with all project stakeholders, across all teams, and deliver results that met their expectations. I was acutely aware of the severe penalties that would be incurred if we experienced any delays on the project and it went beyond the final acceptance date. The pressure was on, and I needed to provide technical responses, nurture teamwork, and build relationships.

With so much at stake, I remained focused on the task at hand, ensuring that every aspect of the project was completed on time based on priorities. Despite the pressure, I was determined to succeed, work hard, build relationships with my colleagues, and deliver results that exceeded the client's expectations. Through hard work, perseverance, and a willingness to learn, I was confident that I would develop the skills I needed to succeed in this and future projects.

4. Adapting to Japanese Business Culture

After the project kickoff meeting on day one in Japan, I felt a sense of relief that it had gone well. However, I knew there was still a lot of learning to do. The first few days of the project went smoothly, and I felt confident in my ability to navigate the cultural differences between Japan and the United States. However, on the third day, in a status-update meeting, I made a crucial error while discussing an urgent telecommunications engineering issue that required immediate attention. I said something that angered one of the client's top senior managers, causing tension to fill the room. Even my colleagues were disappointed with my response.

The meeting took place in a grand conference room filled with state-of-the-art technology and comfortable, high-quality chairs. I sat with my English-Japanese interpreter and local colleagues on one side of the long table, facing the client's team on the other side, and our seating arrangement was based on seniority.

After the meeting, the client's senior manager requested to speak with me privately through an interpreter. He explained that I needed to understand Japanese business culture before working in Japan and quoted a phrase that stuck with me: "Nothing is impossible, but everything is difficult." He taught me that instead of seeing a problem as impossible to solve, we should see it as merely difficult and continue trying to solve it until a solution was found.

He mentioned that when I had responded to the urgent issue by saying it was impossible to resolve, it gave the impression that we had given up on trying to find a solution, but that wasn't true. It was the way I communicated my response that made him think we had given up on the issue.

I saw his point, so I apologized for my miscommunication and let him know that we would continue to investigate the problem and to work towards a solution. I assured him we wouldn't give up and would no longer say it is impossible to resolve.

From that day on, I made a conscious effort to adapt to Japanese work culture. The experience taught me the importance of understanding cultural differences, meeting client expectations, and effectively communicating with them in order to succeed. Ultimately, this experience taught me the importance of acknowledging mistakes and being open to learning, which helped me establish trust and build better relationships with the members of the client team in Japan.

5. Managing Cross-Cultural Relationships in the Workplace

I received frequent emails from my colleagues in Japan, even before I ever put my foot down in that country. One of the key cultural differences was revealed in the way their emails were addressed and signed. They addressed me by my first name, and then they signed with their last names. However, when I replied, I addressed them by their last names and signed with my first name.

One of the other cultural differences was the way the Japanese referred to each other in business and professional environments. The Japanese, regardless of gender or marital status, call each other by their last names, adding the suffix –san. Even when talking about people not present, they add the suffix –san. They addressed their email to me as Nilesh-san. I didn't require that they add –san after my name, but for them it was customary, a sign of respect, polite, and a form of Japanese courtesy to refer to people the correct way.

My frequent use of the suffix –san began when I met Hiroshi in person during one of my first projects in Japan. I called him Hiroshi-san. I was there on a special project to lead a telecommunication project that involved different systems and software applications, for which Hiroshi was the on-site technical engineer. My job was to get the project ready for client acceptance before the commercial launch, and Hiroshi would then support the post-launch activities in commercial sites.

Hiroshi was quite a man, an intelligent and modest man with years of working experience in telecommunications networks and systems. I often considered him my mentor. I felt closest to him. We worked together with great respect. We enjoyed the partnership and friendship developed while working on many challenging and successful project deliveries during my years in Japan.

However, in the beginning, our relationship was anything but a success. He did little to alleviate the mounting pressure I felt as lead on a project that was required to deliver results for the most valued global client that our company had at the time. Early on, it was Hiroshi's resistance to change that made my job very difficult. From the beginning, he was totally uncooperative. I immediately felt rejected, ignored, and discouraged by his behavior towards me. He rarely spoke more than a few words to me.

I had hoped that working with Hiroshi would offer me a learning opportunity, that he would teach me about work-life practices in Japan, that he would share his ideas on how we needed to work and communicate with the client effectively, and that he would give me some personal insights and scouting reports on the different personalities and characters of the client's senior managers and engineers. I thought the more I knew about the people I would be answering questions for, interacting with, and providing daily reports on the project, the better I would perform at my job, and the more productive I would be.

Instead, I sensed by the look on Hiroshi's face and from his body language that he wasn't pleased with me. He didn't think I had the qualifications and experience to work on the project in Japan. When we were in a meeting with the client's team, if they had difficult technical engineering questions for me that I couldn't answer, I often turned around and looked to Hiroshi, hoping he would come to my rescue and assist in explaining or responding to the questions. Instead, I got his silent stare, one that challenged me to respond to the client's technical questions. I felt Hiroshi did this just so he could satisfy his own perceptions about my not being the right person for the job. I felt disappointed by this. I expected us to work together as colleagues and partners. After all, we were working for the same company.

I was young, naïve, and expecting a lot from Hiroshi. He was caught up in his own complex situation and the stereotype in his own imagination. He was hoping someone else from my team in the US—someone better, someone with deeper technical expertise—would show up and replace me.

However, I was determined not to give up on my responsibilities. I knew deep down that, no matter how discouraged I felt, I was endowed with great strength and determination to overcome any challenge in front of me. I had the inner confidence that I was the right person for the job. I was totally focused and concentrated on the project and would do what I needed to do. I listened and adapted to different personalities. I put in tremendous effort and long hours in learning, growing, multitasking, getting better, and keeping my attitude positive.

I had faced many rejections in the past, but this was a very difficult one to swallow because it was coming from my own colleague in another country. Even then, I wasn't going to allow a rejection to hold me back from what I needed to do to achieve success. In fact, I used rejection as a motivator to make great strides in my own progress and growth.

I wasn't going to run away from Hiroshi or from his misbehavior towards me. Much the opposite, I wanted to stay close to him without reacting and criticizing him in return. I didn't want to show my frustration and anger at him, as that would mean weakness on my part. My ability to accept Hiroshi as he was, not as I wanted him to be, showed how much I had grown and matured in a very short time. Although his actions were mean-spirited, insulting, and offensive, I never allowed his negative intentions to bother me. I looked beyond them and stayed positive. I instead focused on his good qualities, which were most needed for the success of the project. I saw a man with intelligence, skills, experience, and wisdom. Hiroshi also embodied great knowledge and insights on innovative telecommunications networking systems.

Hiroshi didn't talk a lot, and he wasn't a very open person. He always came to work on time, totally prepared and focused on his tasks, and did most of his talking by his actions. He liked to be left alone to do his own thing. I often spent time observing how Hiroshi worked with senior managers and members of the client's engineering team. He acted and communicated with friendliness, loyalty, commitment, trustworthiness, and dependability, which I thought were the essential qualities that I needed to embrace and improve upon in my interpersonal relationships and communications with the Japanese client.

After almost eight years of working together on various projects—and, at best, Hiroshi merely putting up with me—we truly became close personal friends and colleagues. It was painful for Hiroshi to accept my role and responsibility in the beginning, but he got over it as time passed. I proved to him through hard work, trust, consistency, and commitment that I was serious about my job. With his quiet and nonverbal nature, and my assertive, social, and problem-solving nature, we were true partners in all of our successes—small, large, and complex projects.

The turning point for us came when Hiroshi invited me to join him for lunch at a popular Japanese restaurant, which was within walking distance of the client's office building. I was so happy and excited that he was opening up. From that day forward, whenever I was in Tokyo on a business trip and working with him, he waited for me to finish whatever I was working on, and then we went to lunch together and shared stories. Sometimes other colleagues joined us for lunch too. Only occasionally did I miss lunch with him because of an urgent work situation or an afternoon meeting with the client. Hiroshi took me to different popular traditional Japanese restaurants, and sometimes recommended a non-Japanese restaurant. We compromised on our choice of restaurants and enjoyed friendly meals together. We both loved Japanese noodles and Indian food, talked casually, and shared many laughs.

In the end, Hiroshi and I worked tirelessly, were always on the same page, and spoke with one clear voice when it came to responding to questions and working with an amazing group of talented engineers, experienced senior managers, and executives on the client's team. We compromised on solutions, exchanged ideas, and delivered on our promises to the client. We knew when to commit and when not to over-commit. He allowed me to take the lead when I was expected to, and he took the lead when he needed to do so.

What I remember the most about Hiroshi was his personality, friendliness, loyalty, responsibility, and dependability. I always felt his presence and knew that he would be there to support me or cover my mistakes while working on the front line with the client's demanding and intelligent engineering staff.

6. Navigating Cross-Cultural Communication and Building Trust

It's a common practice in Japan for businesses to hire Japanese and English interpreters to navigate cultural and linguistic hurdles during business dealings with foreigners. Japan's unique traditions and long history make it essential to avoid cross-cultural misunderstandings and facilitate communication during business meetings, problem-solving, and contract negotiations. The primary focus is on building relationships and trust, and accurate communication is vital.

Having a good relationship with the person translating for me was important to ensure adherence to Japanese cultural etiquette and avoid language hurdles. I first met Nimi at work in Chicago. She was a highly qualified Japan-English interpreter with a friendly, professional, kind, and enthusiastic personality. Nimi was part of a team of Japanese engineers who came to Chicago for a large project meeting, serving as their Japan-English interpreter. Initially, we only interacted during project business meetings in Chicago and in Tokyo. Over the years, we gradually built our trust and friendship. Today, she is a Tokyo-based English and Japanese interpreter, a communications specialist, and a bestselling author.

When we first met, Nimi was early in her career, and I was inexperienced at working through an interpreter. During presentations related to a project or responding to a client's questions, I sometimes talked too long and didn't pause at the right moment for effective translation. My natural flow of thoughts made it challenging to maintain concentration while frequently interrupting myself. I sensed that the managers and engineers on the client's side were becoming frustrated with my lengthy sentences. This situation presented a significant challenge for both Nimi and me.

To avoid confusion, we made extra efforts to go over a quick summary of what was discussed and decided in the meeting, and to answer any remaining questions. This allowed us to work more closely and effectively bridge our language barriers. As time passed, we became proficient at handling our communications in both formal and informal conversations with our client's team members. Nimi adjusted to my personality and style of verbal communication, which helped her do her job more effectively and bring clarity to our client. I always felt a sense of formality when doing business in Japan and wanted to maintain their cultural norms to convey professionalism and respect at all times, and Nimi greatly helped me in this effort.

Although our careers have taken us in different directions since we first worked together, Nimi and I have maintained a strong friendship. We make a point of catching up whenever I'm in Japan, and our conversations are always uplifting and lively. It's a testament to the bond we have formed over the years, one built on mutual respect and a shared appreciation.

7. A Tale of Business, Leadership, and Cultural Differences

As the winter chill settled in, I was excited to hear about an opportunity to provide on-site support at our client's testing center in Makuhari, a vibrant business district outside of Tokyo. Home to a convention center, shopping malls, restaurants, and numerous global corporate offices. Our local team had requested my support to manage and oversee the initial testing of a new project, which involved a large and complex telecommunications system with intricate software applications.

Although I was new to the project and had only worked on it briefly when my Japanese colleagues visited our company's testing center in the United States, my manager assigned me to work with them to show our support and to learn about the new system's applications and functionalities. After over a month, they returned to Japan. Soon after, I began planning and preparing to go to Japan for on-site support, as I had done many times before. The experience of learning and working with our client and my colleagues in Japan was unlike anything I'd been involved in before; it helped me grow professionally in ways I never expected.

As I arrived in Makuhari, Tokyo, where the client's systems testing center was located, I was filled with excitement for the opportunity to work with our local Japanese team and the client's engineering team. They welcomed me back and were thrilled to see me there.

After our first project kickoff meeting with our client's management and engineering teams, the systems verification testing was started by our client. Later in the day, I was informed some basic systems verification testing had failed, which I wasn't expecting on day one. It was terrible news for us about a highly anticipated project for our company. I kept calm and focused on finding more information. I met with my Japanese colleagues to understand the details of the issues.

The manager leading the project from the client's side asked to speak with me in private. It was his low tone of voice that conveyed the pressure and severity of the situation. Failure meant trouble for him and his team for failing to ensure the quality of the system before it was delivered to their test center in Japan. The way he spoke with direct eye contact—he meant it. I understood exactly what he was saying. It was a common practice in Japanese companies to demote, transfer, or fire managers who failed at an assigned task.

Before communicating with my team and other teams in the United States to explain the situation and the client's concerns and expectations, I met with my Japanese colleagues to understand the details of the issues and what type of support was needed from the development team. I also began discussions with the client's middle and senior-level managers to see if we could negotiate a way out of the situation. I had a good relationship with many of these managers, as well as our company's sales and engineering teams in Japan, due to my work on previous projects there. This made it easy for me to have an open, informal, and honest discussion with the client regarding their concerns. My hope was to find a solution that would avoid further delays, costly penalties for delivering an incomplete system, and maintain a positive relationship with the client.

The Japanese are known for being detail-oriented and for asking a lot of questions, which made resolving the issues challenging and delicate. I worked closely with both the client's team and our local team to find solutions on-site and acted as a liaison between functional teams across multiple countries.

As the days wore on, the client's expectations remained high, and tensions mounted as we tried to find a way to turn the project around. I was fortunate to have formed good relationships with both the client's team and our local team in Japan, which helped me navigate the cultural differences and find a way forward.

But just as we thought we had found a solution; I received a call from my manager asking me to return to Chicago. I couldn't comprehend why I was being pulled out of Japan in the middle of the project when it still needed my support. I knew it would cause a major credibility issue with the client and jeopardize our future contracts.

I reached out to the director of my department because he had a good relationship with the senior management of our client and understood the Japanese business culture. I expressed my concerns and asked for his guidance on how to continue supporting the client and how to communicate with them if I were to be pulled out of the project. He then told me that he would speak to my manager and the business division's directors to secure funding to cover my extended stay.

The next day, he informed me that he had spoken to my manager, and they had secured the funding and encouraged me to continue my support for the client's needs in order to resolve all the issues. I extended my stay in Japan and led the project across multiple countries, coordinating with all levels of management and technical team members involved in the project, providing necessary facts and data to help find solutions.

The experience was a perfect storm of business, leadership, and cultural differences, but it taught me valuable lessons in navigating office politics, managing complex projects, and leading through challenging times. By staying focused on the client's needs and taking one day at a time, I was able to deliver on my promises and help turn the project around.

This experience reminded me of the importance of building strong relationships with colleagues and clients, understanding cultural differences, and never giving up in the face of adversity. While there were sacrifices made along the way, I did it willingly and because it was the right thing to do. And in the end, it paid off with a successful project, happy client, and valuable lessons learned.

Although I had been to Japan on business many times in the previous years, this was a special experience that brought some of my hidden talents and skills to the surface as I was leading and managing a very complex multimillion-dollar project involving talented and experienced engineers and managers from around the world. The challenges and pressures were immense. Had I not already learned valuable lessons in building relationships and effectively communicating and negotiating solutions, the outcome could have been vastly different and disastrous for our company.

In conclusion, this experience taught me valuable lessons about cross-cultural communication, leadership, and perseverance. I ended up staying in Japan for over six months, staying focused on the client's needs, working closely with all stakeholders, and taking initiative, I was able to lead a complex project to success. It also highlights the importance of understanding the dynamics of management and office politics, while staying true to one's values and principles.

8. Being a Leader Means Being Open to New Possibilities

By this time, I had been in Japan for more than six months, which was one of my longest business trips there. My initial plan was to be there for only two weeks for on-site support. I wasn't an expert on the complex telecommunications system with multiple software applications, so I wasn't expected to know a lot about it. We had jointly agreed that the local team members were the key experts and that they would primarily support the first phase of system testing in the customer's testing center.

Little did I know that my extended stay in Japan would be accompanied by unexpected challenges. The dynamic nature of my job often presented unexpected hurdles during business trips. It wasn't the first time that things didn't go as planned, with deliverables and deadlines constantly evolving. As a result, I had to remain flexible and responsive, ready to adapt and extend my stay in Japan to overcome these obstacles and ensure the success of the project.

Once I was informed that the basic functionality of the features and applications had failed, I had to communicate the bad news to my manager, directors, and senior executives from various organizations in the United States, explaining the current state of the system and the client's expectations. Our client was the Japan's largest and most reputed telecommunications carrier in the world, making this a critical project for us. Our company's reputation and future contracts were at stake. Not to mention that the test failure meant we were going to miss the client's target acceptance date and would be forced to pay large financial penalties to the client as a result.

The client asked our company's senior management team to come in person and explain the situation and to describe in detail our plan to resolve the issues found. They also asked that I remain in Japan until all the issues were resolved. So as my originally planned business trip was getting close to an end, and while I was caught up in the chaos and under the pressure of trying to manage all the on-site issues, I got a call from my manager. Instead of accommodating the client's urgent needs and understanding their request, my manager requested that I return home despite my efforts to resolve the issues. He had someone else in mind to support the remainder of the project, without considering the implications for the client or our company's reputation. This was unexpected in the business culture of Japan, where customer satisfaction and relationship building are highly valued.

Risking my manager's ire, I went to our director, with whom I had a good relationship, and expressed my concerns. Pulling me out of Japan so soon, in direct opposition to the client's expressed wishes, would make the client even more unhappy with us. Both the director and I knew the impact it would have on the project if I left without sufficient reason; it would cause a major credibility issue. My director spoke to my manager about the situation and the next day they were able to secure the necessary funds to cover my travel expenses so that I could stay in Japan until all the system-wide issues were resolved.

My manager was displeased with my decision to escalate the issue to our director. I was concerned about the potential difficulties that could arise with our relationship with our client from pulling me out of the project amidst the chaos. He was only seeing things from his perspective and not how this client worked and associated risk factors and trust. Nevertheless, I remained focused on steering the project as I was asked to continue in a positive direction. I started leading the project across all engineering teams in the US, Japan, China, and India, communicating with all senior and low-level managers and technical members involved in the project, providing all the necessary facts, scenarios, and data of each issue—all in the hopes of a quick turnaround through software patches. My two weeks turned into more than a six months' stay in Japan. Other colleagues from my team joined me in the latter stages of the project, but I remained the main point of contact.

I have always believed in providing excellent client service. It's important for an organization to consider the customer's perspective and to listen to their needs and priorities when making planning decisions, even if that involves additional travel costs or adding resources to meet their immediate needs. As a result, the client will see how committed we are to their success, and that always brings rewards.

Reflecting back on my experience leading this project, I realized that being a leader means being open to new possibilities and being able to adapt to unexpected changes. It means having the courage to take risks and to make difficult decisions. It also means being able to form relation-ships with people from different cultures and backgrounds and being able to communicate effectively with them. This project taught me a lot about leadership and myself, and I will always be grateful for the opportunity to have led such a successful and memorable project.

9. A Memorable Evening of Celebration in Tokyo

I vividly recall an unforgettable evening in Tokyo, filled with joy and accomplishment. It marked the successful completion of one of the most complex and expensive telecom engineering projects I had ever led on-site in Japan. Our team and the customer's team came together in a joint celebration, expressing gratitude and recognizing the hard work of our colleagues. We shared heartfelt speeches, indulged in delicious food and drinks, and enjoyed the lively atmosphere. This celebration holds a special place in my memory, not only because of the project's success but also because it marked my longest stay in Japan during a single trip.

We were dressed in business attire. Business dinners are always an integral part of professional life in Japan. They are essential to building relationships with customers and colleagues. It was an amazing evening of laughs and joy with people whom I had grown to respect over the years. We shared quality time together and told a lot of happy stories.

The dinner was at a traditional Japanese restaurant in a popular area of Tokyo. The atmosphere was calm, there was little foot traffic, and we were surrounded by short and long, rectangular, black and white signs bearing the names of other restaurants in Japanese characters. On the side of the street were some parked motorcycles and bicycles, while occasionally one of Tokyo's famous green-and-yellow taxis went by; they are known for their cleanliness and are very expensive. Upon entering the restaurant, I noticed the usual clear-glass window display revealing wax replicas of the restaurant's food. The display was visually perfect, and each dish was accompanied by an accurate description and price; it was there to attract and inform customers of the restaurant's menu. It was a very helpful illustration of the type of food that they served, especially for someone, like me, who didn't read and speak Japanese. When I was at these types of traditional Japanese restaurants, I quietly requested a waiter or waitress kindly step to the display so that I could point to the food I wanted to order. It made it much easier.

Just as we entered the restaurant—which was a low-ceiling wooden structure with perfect evening lighting for a comfortable dining experience—we were greeted with a loud, "Irasshaimase," meaning, "Welcome, please come in." This was a traditional low-table Japanese restaurant. The waiter in a low voice very kindly and politely asked us how many people were in our party and to remove our shoes at the entrance before stepping into the restaurant, which is a very common practice in Japan. The waiter then graciously directed us to a table, where we sat on pillow seats on the floor, and gave us menus. Although I couldn't read the menu, the people who had organized the dinner ordered a variety of small dishes to meet everyone's needs.

I had been in other Japanese restaurants that had Western-style tables and chairs, but the traditional Japanese sit on the floor. At first, I was uncomfortable sitting on the floor, but I got used to it after a while. I had gone to dinners where they had a special dining room with a sliding wooden door for an intimate and private setting for a group of friends or colleagues. This offered fascinating and unique exposure to the beautiful traditional culture and customs of dining in Japan.

Reflecting on that evening, I realize that it wasn't just the successful completion of the project that made it so special. It was also the opportunity to celebrate with my colleagues and the chance to experience the culture and traditions of Japan. Through my work and my travels, I have learned that the most important part of any project is the people who work on it. Building strong relationships and treating others with respect is essential to achieving success, not just in business, but in life. And so, as I look back on that night, I'm reminded of the valuable lessons I have learned, the memories I have made, and the friendships that will last a lifetime.

10. The Impact of a Boss on Your Career

Your boss can be the key to unlocking your potential in the workplace. I have had many bosses throughout my career, and I realize how important it is to have a good one. Unfortunately, they come with various personalities and management styles.

The boss that still stands out in my career was my first boss who hired me as a telecommunications engineer right after college. He had amazing leadership qualities and wasn't just a good boss, but also a great person. With his focus on team support and a positive work environment, he instilled confidence and trust in us to do the right thing and work together.

He never allowed me to feel inferior to the senior engineers who had more technical experience than I, and always gave me opportunities to learn from them. He took risks on me, and even assigned me a critical project that required onsite support in Japan, even though I was still learning about the company's systems and technology. He mentored me and guided me on the right path to becoming a productive engineer for the team.

He was tough when he had to be, and he let me know if I wasn't performing well. He motivated me to seek higher education and approved employee tuition reimbursement so I could pursue a master's degree in computer science as a part-time graduate student. He allowed flexible work time when I needed it to focus on my exams, and he encouraged me to take up hobbies outside of work. He helped me improve my communication and business-writing skills by letting me get the training I needed, making me give presentations to the team, and proofreading my emails before sending them to our client's team. He even helped me set up a long-term savings account, like a 401K, when I didn't know what it was, and reminded me to keep my financial status healthy.

One time, while I was in Japan for a project, my boss called me to see how things were going. He could sense the pressure and tension in my tone from working long hours, not getting enough sleep, and trying to meet the client's expectations. Instead of just asking about the project, he kept the conversation light and friendly, even sharing some food places that I should check out to help me relax. He asserted that I was doing a good job and urged me to take it easy and take care of myself. It was great to have a boss who cared about me as a person; it made me feel valued, not just as an employee, but also as a human being.

On the other hand, I have had bad bosses. The bad ones all shared similar personalities and traits. The one that first comes to mind was so biased and insecure. He micromanaged everything I did and criticized me for what I wasn't doing right, instead of recognizing what I was doing correctly. Even when I achieved a successful project result, he credited someone else on our team or said they did it better. When I showed initiative and excitement about leading a new project, he turned me down and assigned me something with less visibility in the department and fewer growth opportunities. He always compared me to people with years of experience and assigned me projects with little opportunity for growth or development.

When I asked for additional training courses or outside training for personal and professional development, he questioned my motives. He changed his mind at the last minute on projects and assignments, leaving me unsure of what to do. He gave preferential treatment to certain team members and ignored others, which led to a toxic work environment. He intentionally took away opportunities for growth and development, assigning projects to his favorites and leaving others with little to do. He was also untrustworthy, saying one thing to me, but something else to a coworker, creating confusion and tension within the team. When I volunteered outside of work and shared my experiences from the networking event, he didn't care to hear any details.

It's important to get to know your bosses and their characters, as they have significant influence over your career. While it's important to work with them to achieve success and to strive to please them, it's also crucial to take the initiative and showcase our skills to top management.

Personal motivation and bias by a boss can prevent us from growing to our true potential. Engaging in any political behavior by a boss can be counterproductive to our success at work. Seeking out mentors and opportunities for growth and development can help to overcome the challenges posed by a bad boss.

Overall, having a good boss can make a world of difference in our careers, and it's important that we strive to find one who supports our growth and development. When we recognize that our boss doesn't have our best interests at heart, it's best to quickly make a switch to another position not under that boss's management. If such a position does not exist within your organization, you may have to seek employment elsewhere. Asking for feedback from colleagues working under the boss with whom you are having trouble can help you make an informed decision.

However, it's important to remember that not all bosses will be perfect, and it's our responsibility to take owner-ship of our careers and work towards our goals, Despite the challenges, we must remain proactive and determined to achieve success.

Discoveries in Japan:
Success, Bonds, and Beyond

1. Navigating Tokyo's Commute: A Lesson in Perseverance and Adaptability

When I arrived at my hotel in Tokyo after a long fourteen-hour international flight from the United States, I was thrilled to be back in the city. This was my second business trip to Japan to support a complex technical assignment for the same client. This time around, I was less concerned about airport logistics and more excited to see my local colleagues and the members of the client's team. Despite this, I still felt a twinge of nervousness about the challenges that awaited me, the scrutiny I would be under, and the pressure to successfully complete the project.

On this trip, I stayed at a luxurious hotel located in Akasaka, in the heart of Tokyo. It was one of the best hotels in the city, with stunning architecture that impressed me from the moment I saw it. The white tower stood tall, with thirty-seven floors, large glass windows, and 844 rooms.

The main entrance had a large waiting and guest-pickup area for taxis. The lobby was spacious; it had high ceilings and an impressive welcome area, as well as dining areas, cafes, lounges, a small bakery, and escalators. The hotel's warm, classic Japanese contemporary design was elegantly decorated with hanging light fixtures that evoked the spirit of Japanese decor. The tables and chairs were of traditional red, orange, and brown colors that beautifully complemented the warm colors on the walls.

One thing that stood out for me was how the hotel smartly optimized the space using minimal furnishings. The prestigious Tokyo hotel had something for everyone, including a shopping arcade, banquet halls, conference rooms, and a wide variety of restaurants. The staff was courteous, willing, and eager to serve. They were accommodating and spoke English, which was really helpful. The rooms were clean and comfortable; they had low lighting and natural decor, and offered spectacular views of the Tokyo skyline, both during the day and night.

The hotel's location was perfect for me. It was a long distance from the client's office, but it was within walking distance of my company's local office building located in Akasaka. The area was clean, safe, and peaceful, with easy access to the underground train and city bus stations. Not only was the hotel conveniently located near my company's office, but the surrounding area also offered a multitude of attractions and amenities. The embassies of the United States, Canada, Mexico, and Spain were located nearby, along with Tokyo Midtown, which is the tallest high-rise complex in Tokyo. The area also housed major Japanese and international company headquarters, offices of various airlines, local restaurants, convenience stores, shops, schools, libraries, and even a small police station.

On the evening of my arrival, despite feeling tired from the long flight and needing food and rest, I decided to get familiar with the surrounding area and plan my commute for the next morning. I consulted with the hotel concierge, who was very polite and friendly. He assisted me by providing maps of the city, including information on the bus system, subway routes, and the Japan Railways intercity rail service (the JR Line). He informed me that the train and bus were the most affordable, commonly used, and quickest ways of traveling, considering how expensive taxi rides were in Tokyo. According to him, I had a one-and-a-half-hour train commute to reach my client's office in Makuhari, a commercial district located just outside central Tokyo. Although my commute time was above average, I wasn't surprised, as I knew from my previous trip that long commutes are common in Tokyo.

My first memorable experience came when I took a walk around the hotel area. I had not really seen or experienced being in any big international city other than Tokyo. The atmosphere was lively and vibrant. The air was fresh and clean, and the sidewalks were packed with Japanese people walking fast and dressed in fashionable formal clothing. The roads were busy with heavy traffic, including taxis, cars, buses, trucks, and motorcycles. There were traditional cyclists on bicycle paths and people in beautifully colored kimonos. It was amazing!

The next morning, I woke up early, had a light breakfast, and got dressed in a black business suit with a bright-colored tie. I started walking towards the nearby subway station. It was morning rush hour, and there was a long line of Japanese people waiting to get on the train. The station was one of the busiest in Tokyo, and there were a few hundred people all moving at the same time in both directions.

The stairs were designed to handle large crowds, and some people were coming up, while others were going down. The commuters were moving at great speed; some were even running. Men wore leather shoes, some women wore high heels, and there were a few people carrying umbrellas. The commuters were in their own world, not speaking to one another, and focused on where they needed to go.

In the station, there were also a large café, a busy convenience store, a shoe-repair shop, and kiosks selling candy, newspapers, magazines, and books. There was even a large public mirror just beside the entrance gate, which busy commuters used to fix their hair or put the final touches on their makeup.

My first challenge of the morning came when I had to purchase a subway ticket. I didn't know how to do that or even how much it cost. I observed how the commuters were doing it and saw that they were inserting money into a ticket-vending machine until the fare button lit up. After entering an amount, a ticket and change came out at the bottom of the machine. Before purchasing my ticket, I needed to locate the fare for my end destination.

Ticket fares were posted on a large subway map near the ticket-vending machines, but the station names were listed in Japanese. I asked a couple of people for help, but they couldn't speak English. So, I walked over to a station attendant for help, but he didn't speak English either. I showed him my subway map in English and pointed to where I wanted to go. He then quickly used his calculator and manually typed in 160, which was my fare. After I bought my ticket and went through the train gates, I headed for the platform for the trains headed in the direction of my destination.

During the crowded train ride, there was hardly any room left to stand, resulting in physical discomfort. The motion of the train forcibly moved my body from one side of the door to the other, and I was continuously pushed around amidst a sea of other passengers. I found myself in close proximity, face-to-face with fellow commuters. At one point, I became pressed against the door and unable to move freely.

Although I felt uncomfortable, I was amazed by the efficiency and orderliness of the Japanese train system. It was incredible to see how the train attendants could quickly and safely get all the passengers on and off the trains. They literally pushed people onto the train until everyone could fit inside and the doors could be safely closed.

Once inside, passengers traveled in total silence, reading, browsing their mobile devices or just staring straight ahead, giving each other privacy. Despite the crowded conditions, the people were exceptionally polite and considerate. It was a fascinating and unforgettable experience to witness the Japanese manners and be part of such a unique and organized transportation system.

I made it to the client's office building after a long journey that took over an hour and a half. Although it was tiring and exhausting, I was proud to have made it in time for my first project kickoff meeting. However, a few days later, I encountered another challenge when I mistakenly took the wrong train on the Japan Railways intercity route. This experience taught me valuable life lessons about making quick decisions when dealing with unexpected situations, staying vigilant, and being persistent when encountering and adapting to real-time challenges.

I mistakenly took the wrong train towards our client's office. I had to ask around to find the right station, but unfortunately most people I encountered didn't speak English. Adding to the difficulty, I didn't have a mobile phone that worked in Japan, which meant I couldn't call my colleagues for assistance or notify them about the delay. I was particularly worried about missing the daily morning status meeting with the client's team and leaving them wondering about my absence. However, I managed to find a public pay phone available at the train station. I dialed my colleague's number and explained the situation, informing him of the delay and the reasons behind it.

Finally, after a long day of work, I headed back to the hotel by taking two train systems during the evening rush hour, the Tokyo metro underground subway and the Japan Railways. Both were more crowded than in the morning. I had to endure the same challenges of being in crowded trains and finding the right connections. However, I had gained some experience and confidence in navigating the transportation system, so I was able to handle it better than on my morning commute.

A few days later, as I got off the train, I felt a sense of relief and accomplishment. I had successfully completed my daily commute in Tokyo for several days, and it had become somewhat routine for me. I was even starting to recognize some familiar faces on the train and at the station. I also began to notice some of the small details that make commuting in Tokyo unique, such as the cleanliness of the trains and stations, the efficiency of the transportation system, and the unwritten rules of etiquette that everyone seemed to follow.

Despite the challenges, I found myself appreciating the experience of commuting in Tokyo. It was a window into the everyday lives of the people who lived and worked in Tokyo. The journey to and from work became a time for me to observe and learn about the local culture and customs, and to reflect on my own experiences and challenges.

Overall, my daily commute in Tokyo taught me valuable lessons about patience, perseverance, and adaptability. It helped me to develop a greater appreciation for the complexity and diversity of the world we live in. And, most importantly, it gave me the confidence to navigate new challenges and adventures, no matter how daunting they may seem at first.

2. Navigating Unexpected Situations while Working in Japan

Friday evenings in Japan, it's common for colleagues and friends to socialize after work, and I was no exception. One summer, I found myself in Tokyo, working at a client's office building testing center. I had originally planned to meet some colleagues for dinner in central Tokyo. However, at the last minute, one of the senior managers of the client's team kindly invited me to join them for dinner, an invitation I couldn't refuse.

The restaurant was on the top floor of a twenty-six-story in the client's building, offering a stunning view of Tokyo Bay in the Chiba Prefecture. The atmosphere was lively and relaxed as people chatted and enjoyed their conversations.

Being a vegetarian, I ordered plain steamed rice. Unfortunately, when it arrived, it was cold and mixed with tiny pieces of pork. Not wanting to make a fuss and distract everyone, I said nothing and sat quietly. However, some members of the client's team noticed that I wasn't eating and asked me why. When I explained the situation, they apologized and had the waitress bring me a new plate of plain, hot, steamy white rice. Unfortunately, even that wasn't enough to prevent what happened next.

Later that night, as I was getting ready for a late dinner with my colleagues, I suddenly experienced extreme abdominal cramping, weakness, and dizziness. I was intensely nauseated and began vomiting. I could barely stand, and my eyes kept closing. It was clear I needed medical attention, but I didn't know where to turn. I contacted the hotel manager, who quickly sprang into action and arranged for an English-speaking doctor to visit me the next morning.

I was diagnosed with severe food poisoning from steamed rice, and the doctor prescribed medication and rest. The hotel manager was incredibly kind and attentive, checking on me every hour and bringing me water and juice to stay hydrated throughout the night.

Although I eventually recovered, the experience taught me the importance of being cautious when traveling abroad. I learned to only eat freshly cooked food served hot, drink water or juice from sealed bottles, and avoid undercooked food at restaurants.

But the experience also showed me the true humanity and kindness of the Japanese people. The hotel manager went above and beyond to care for me, and the members of the client's team were sincerely apologetic, even though they had no control over what happened.

The memory of that night in Tokyo remains with me to this day. It was a time of both challenge and growth; I had to rely on the kindness of strangers to get through a difficult situation. I learned the value of building relationships with colleagues and local staff, as their support can be crucial in times of need. It also showed me the beauty of Japanese culture, with its emphasis on group harmony and taking care of others.

This experience also deepened my appreciation for the importance of health and self-care while on the road. Whenever I travel abroad now, I make sure to research local customs and become aware of food choices before arriving at a new destination or trying unfamiliar food options.

Working internationally can present challenges and unexpected obstacles, but it has also given me some of the most rewarding experiences of my life. I have learned to stay calm in difficult situations, ask for help when needed, and learn from each experience. Working with diverse cultures has made me more open-minded, given me new interpersonal skills, and taught me how to adapt to new situations and be open to unexpected events. Through my exposure to the global market, I have built relationships across cultures and gained a broader perspective about the world. I'm grateful for the lessons I have learned and the memories I have made along the way.

3. Building Cross-Cultural Relationships: A Journey of Making Friends Abroad

In my early years of traveling to Tokyo, making friends on business trips was incredibly difficult. Being away from home, family, and friends was tough. As a social person who enjoys engaging in conversations with people, it was uncomfortable being alone in such a large city.

During those days, I was a frequent business traveler to Japan in those days, spending anywhere from two weeks to a couple of months away from home. The work was very exhausting and stressful, with twelve-hour days being the norm in Japan. The demanding schedule and lack of free time to socialize and make friends made it difficult to build meaningful relationships outside of work. I often felt alone and had no friends to speak with or share my daily experiences with when I finished work.

The days during the week passed by quickly, leaving only late nights or weekends as free time. Unfortunately, this free time was often interrupted by unexpected phone calls from family, managers, or late-night conference calls requested by colleagues in the US. I stayed up late or found free time on the weekend to send follow-up emails on the problems found during software, hardware, or data testing by the client's engineering team. Sometimes I took on additional roles, verifying and sending follow-up emails on documentation, giving advice, and getting involved in other contractual obligations.

I found it challenging to strike a healthy balance between work, personal time, and recreational activities. Although I connected with a few colleagues who were on long-term expatriate assignments, our interactions still felt more work-related. I craved friendships with like-minded individuals who shared common interests. Realizing that no one was going to do this for me, I made a deliberate effort to attend local social or professional networking events on weekends, which I found by reading local newspapers and magazines.

Tokyo is an international city with people from all over the world living and working there. Attending events organized by foreign organizations and business-networking groups, as well as private events organized by locals or people on long-term business assignments, provided me with the opportunity to meet new people who spoke English, making communication much easier. I exchanged contact information with those whom I felt connected to and made a point to stay in touch with them through email or phone calls. We would often meet for coffee, dinner, or weekend activities, which helped to foster stronger bonds. As my circle of social friends started to grow, they introduced me to their friends, giving me the chance to meet a diverse group of successful professionals from around the world and to learn from them.

Not only did this allow me to create the work-play balance I needed while doing business in Tokyo, but it also provided me with the opportunity to meet warm-hearted, multilingual people eager to help and welcome me into their social circles.

It was a unique and valuable experience that helped me form lasting friendships and broaden my perspective.

As I spent more time in Tokyo, I became increasingly curious and fascinated by the Japanese people, their culture, and traditions. I attended outdoor festivals and other events to learn more about them. However, as most Japanese people were reserved, it was challenging for both sides to communicate and connect. I found it difficult to strike up conversations with strangers, particularly as most Japanese people didn't speak English, and I couldn't speak Japanese.

Despite the language barrier, I persevered and continued to approach strangers, saying, "Konichiwa," and initiate short conversations. I found that the Japanese people were always respectful and gracious, even if they didn't want to talk. They either tried to speak in simple English or used digital translators to communicate.

I remained committed to making Japanese friends whenever I had free time. With persistence, I gained confidence and met a few Japanese people, both men and women, who spoke English. Through these genuine conversations, I learned so much about the Japanese people, their customs, and the Japanese way of life.

Sometimes, conversations didn't flow well due to the language differences, and I could get frustrated and anxious. However, I stayed calm and focused on whatever little connection I had made, hoping to build on it and possibly get the chance to meet again. While some experiences were setbacks and emotionally bruising, I tried to gain insight from each encounter and to develop my ability to make Japanese friends. Over time, I became better at handling rejection and appreciated that every encounter was a new beginning and a learning opportunity. Ultimately, it was much easier for me to adjust to their style of thinking and communication, than for them to adjust to mine.

I didn't have a lot of free time during the week, but I took whatever I had and spent it with these new friends in order to build relationships. Either they invited me, or I invited them, for a walk around shopping districts, such as Shinjuku or Ginza in Tokyo. We met for coffee, lunch, or dinner, and sometimes we visited Tokyo's famous temple in Asakusa, which is one of the most popular tourist destinations in Tokyo, to buy souvenirs and see people of all ages wearing traditional Japanese kimonos.

Making friends in Tokyo was a difficult but rewarding experience. Despite the challenges of language and cultural barriers, I was able to build lasting relationships by being persistent, investing time and energy, and initiating the first contact. Through these friendships, I gained a better understanding of the Japanese people, their culture, and their way of life. This experience taught me the importance of taking the initiative, being open-minded, and embracing differences to form meaningful cross-cultural relationships.

4. Finding Strength in Adversity: A Story of Friendship in Tokyo

I was on a routine business trip to Japan when, one weekend, I went to a social event with my friends in Tokyo. That was where I first met Miko; she was very friendly, sincere, and funny, and she spoke very good English. Although I was busy talking with my friends most of the evening, I remembered Miko very well.

I continued to see Miko from time to time at different social events. Eventually, we began exchanging emails. Miko sent me information about places to visit, things to see, and weekend festivals around Tokyo. During a visit to the popular temple in Asakusa, a district in Tokyo, on a beautiful, sunny day, I had the opportunity to get to know Miko on a more personal level. The temple's rich history and vibrant souvenir shops created a relaxing experience. As we walked around the temple grounds, immersing ourselves in the fascinating history and exploring the colorful array of souvenirs, our friendship deepened. It was a memorable day that strengthened our bond and created lasting memories.

During our next meeting at a cafe, I realized Miko wasn't feeling well. She appeared stressed, physically weak, and uncomfortable, but I couldn't determine the cause. Japanese people are often hesitant to open up about their personal problems. I didn't want to put. Miko on the spot by asking a direct question about it, so we talked about other topics and interests.

Miko disclosed to me that she had been diagnosed with a serious medical condition similar to a tumor and needed to be hospitalized for testing and treatment. Although she didn't share specific details about it, she conveyed the seriousness of her situation. Her courage in sharing such personal information with me was a powerful gesture of trust and vulnerability, and I was honored that she chose to confide in me.

I was taken aback by the news and shocked at how calmly she spoke about it. I asked her more about her diagnosis and treatment plans, assuming that she had the support of her family during this difficult time, but she revealed that her parents, brother, and sister lived far away from Tokyo, and she didn't want to worry them by sharing the news. It seemed as if she just needed someone with whom to talk, and I was the only person she confided in. I felt honored that she trusted me with such a personal decision, and I was determined to support her in any way possible. While I wanted to suggest that Miko contact her family for support, I refrained from doing so. She was already under a lot of stress, and I didn't want to complicate things further. Despite the gravity of her situation, Miko displayed great inner strength and courage. She looked happy, remained positive and enthusiastic, and came to terms with her health situation.

Before she was admitted to the hospital, Miko was extremely nervous about letting her mother know of her situation. It seemed as if she was worried and didn't want to cause her family any pain or stress. I also felt that maybe she was feeling ashamed. Eventually, though, I convinced Miko to tell her mother about her health situation.

Within a few days, her mother traveled to Tokyo from a distant island to be with her. Other family members also came to visit her in the hospital. The fact that they came to support her and stayed with her while she was going through treatment showed they cared for her. Seeing how relieved and happy Miko was to have her family with her, I felt grateful that I could play a small part in helping her through a difficult time.

During her hospital stay, I visited her whenever I could, even though it was an hour-long commute by train from my work outside of Tokyo. Her hospital was located far from my usual train stations, but I made the effort to see her before visiting hours ended, offering her my support and prayers. She only needed someone to help her once she was released from the hospital and to take her to follow-up appointments.

Fortunately, after treatment, all of Miko's tests came back negative, and she was free from any sign of the tumor-like condition. It was happy news for her, her family, and me. She later told me how her family relationships had improved and how her communication with her mother and sister had changed; it opened a new chapter for them.

Life can be unpredictable, and we never know what purpose our friendships and relationships will serve. When I first met Miko at a social event in Tokyo, I couldn't have anticipated the profound impact our friendship would have on my life. Over the years, our connection grew stronger, and we've remained close friends.

Miko's personal struggles taught me a lot about her character. She displayed remarkable bravery, calmness, and courage, even in the face of a serious illness. Despite her worry about how her health would affect her family, she remained positive and optimistic. I wouldn't have discovered these things about her through just our conversations; I was able to see her true character through her actions. Throughout her ordeal of testing and treatment, I never saw her complain, get angry, or blame anyone. Instead, she remained focused on her family and the pain she might cause them. It was inspiring to see someone face such a difficult situation with such grace.

Her experience also gave me a window into Japanese culture and customs. In Japan, it's common to keep private information to oneself, even when it's of the utmost importance. Miko's decision to confide in me was a powerful gesture of trust, and I was honored to be the person in whom she chose to confide.

Through my friendship with Miko, I learned how to face adversity with grace and strength. Her example continues to inspire me to this day.

5. From Spain to Japan: A Friendship Journey

During my travels in Japan, I had the opportunity to meet many wonderful people and form lasting friendships. One such friendship began unexpectedly in Spain, while I was on a trip with a college friend. We were exploring the city of Cordoba and looking for someone to take our picture. We noticed a friendly-looking gentleman dressed in casual clothes. We approached him and asked him to take our photo, and that is when we learned that he was from Japan.

I was excited to meet someone from Japan in Spain, and our brief conversation left me wanting to know more about him. He graciously introduced himself as Saito and gave me his contact information, suggesting that I reach out to him the next time I was in Japan. Little did I know that our chance encounter would lead to a lasting friendship.

A few days later, we ran into each other in Seville, another historical and beautiful city of Spain. This time I was by myself as my college friend had returned to the United States. So, Saito and I walked around the city of Seville and spent time together. We shared common interests and passions for travel, culture, and music. We both loved traveling to different parts of the world, exploring cultures and traditions, and meeting people. We had a great time together, visiting different tourist destinations and walking around the city. We explored the sights and sounds of Seville, its charming neighborhoods, and the local scenery. It was a joy to share this experience with someone who appreciated the local culture as much as I did. We exchanged stories about our travels, our favorite destinations, and our experiences meeting people from around the world.

After our day together, we said our goodbyes, promising to keep in touch. True to his word, my new Japanese friend and I stayed in contact over the years, despite living on opposite sides of the world. We sent each other postcards and messages, sharing updates on our lives and travels. And when I finally returned to Japan, he was there to welcome me and show me around the city.

A year later, I traveled to Tokyo for business and had the pleasure of meeting Saito again. He invited me to join him and his band members at his home on a weekend evening. As a member of a musical band, he played different instruments and traveled the world playing music. That evening, they performed beautiful and harmonious music that was a blend of Japanese, Indian, and Nepalese classical sounds. It was an incredible experience to witness their musical talent and enjoy their music with friends.

During one visit to Tokyo, Saito took me to a hidden gem known as Omoide Yokocho, or Piss Alley, located near the bustling Japan Railways station in Shinjuku, a major district in Tokyo, Japan, renowned for its vibrant shopping and restaurants. The narrow street, barely wide enough for two to pass, was lined with tiny bars and barbecue stands. Saito led me to one of the oldest and most famous Japanese soba-noodle stalls, where I was introduced to this beloved dish. He even taught me how to order soba noodles in traditional Japanese and become a champion at eating the hot and steamy noodles from a large bowl using chopsticks. Soba noodles are made from buckwheat flour and served either hot or cold; the cold variation is served on a tray with a soy-based dipping sauce, and the hot in a bowl of hot, clear broth.

Since our first spontaneous meeting in Spain, our friendship has grown stronger with time. We keep in touch on a regular basis, and I always make sure to meet my friend Saito whenever I visit Tokyo.

These are just a few examples of warm and generous human beings who have had a profound positive impact on my life. My amazing Japanese friends have influenced my personal growth and character in significant ways; they accompanied me to places and festivals where I would have otherwise been alone during my business trips to Tokyo. Through their friendships, I have been able to experience life in Tokyo and gain a deeper understanding of Japanese culture. These unexpected friendships taught me that sometimes the best connections happen in the most unlikely places. By keeping an open mind and being willing to strike up conversations with strangers, I was able to make lasting connections with people from a completely different culture. Their warmth and generosity have left a lasting impact on my life and knowing them continues to inspire me to be a better person. It's a lesson I'll always carry with me as I continue to travel and explore the world.

6. A Lesson in Japanese Punctuality and Hospitality

I had arranged to meet with Saito at a popular crossing in Tokyo, close to my hotel. I shared our story in the previous chapter, where I detailed our friendship and the experiences we had together. I was running late; I had no way of notifying him. I didn't have a cell phone because getting mobile-phone service as a foreigner in Tokyo can be a challenge. I didn't have a mobile phone that worked in Japan then. When I finally arrived at our meeting place, Saito casually reminded me that being late for a meeting is not considered good manners in Japan, even among friends.

On another occasion, it was Saito who was running late for our meeting. However, I didn't have a mobile phone, so he had no means of directly contacting me. Although it was not a big deal for me to wait for him, he was so concerned that he called my hotel, which was a fifteen-minute walk from where I was waiting. He provided my name, description of my appearance, and the street corner where we were supposed to meet to the hotel manager. Saito kindly requested that a staff member be sent to our meeting place to inform me that he was running late. This thoughtful gesture highlighted the depth of Saito's hospitality.

As I waited at the street corner, a Japanese man in a black suit and tie approached me, introducing himself as a staff from the hotel where I was staying. He asked for my name. I was surprised and shocked that the hotel knew where I was and what I looked like. I wondered if something urgent had happened. After I provided my name, he handed me a white envelope with my name and the hotel logo on it. Inside, there was a note from the hotel manager informing me that my friend was running late, apologizing for the delay, and providing an exact new meeting time based on the next train. The train station was conveniently located just around the corner from where I was waiting.

This experience illustrated the importance of punctuality and consideration in Japanese culture. My friend's concern for my well-being extended to contacting my hotel to ensure I was informed of the delay. Such gestures of kindness and thoughtfulness have been common throughout my friendships with Japanese people, leaving a lasting impact on my life.

This experience gave me profound insight into the sharp cultural differences between the Japanese and Americans, instilling in me a profound respect for the Japanese people. I was deeply impressed by Saito's attentiveness and ability to get someone from one of Tokyo's top hotels to walk over fifteen minutes just to deliver a message, in person, that he was running late. What was even more impressive was that the hotel, which prided itself on excellent customer service, actually honored my friend's request and delivered the message. Such exceptional customer service is a testament to the hospitality and dedication that is unique to Japan.

Through this experience, I gained a valuable understanding of the importance of punctuality in Japanese culture. It became clear to me that the Japanese prioritize timeliness and keeping commitments. This incident impressed upon me that it was essential for me to keep my promises and always show up on time, or earlier, if I wanted to build solid relationships with my Japanese friends and business associates. Though from time to time I continued to commit social faux pas due to our cultural differences, my friends were generally forgiving and kind towards me.

7. Kamakura: A Peaceful Retreat for Work-Life Balance

Located about an hour southwest of Tokyo by train, Kamakura is a charming ancient city that was once the political capital of Japan. It's known as the City of Warriors and features deep-green, wooded mountains, Buddhist temples, Shinto shrines, and other historical monuments. Despite being a small city, it's a popular tourist destination due to its many attractions and proximity to the sea.

During the summer months, many travelers visit Kamakura to enjoy mountain trails, swimming, surfing, or just breathing in the clean fresh air on the sandy beach. For those who don't enjoy the sea, the city is filled with beautiful natural gardens that are perfect for a calm and relaxing getaway.

One of Kamakura's most famous sights is the outdoor bronze statue of the Great Buddha, which was cast in the year 1252 during the Kamakura period. The statue is over thirteen meters high and weighs ninety-three tons, making it Japan's second-largest statue of Buddha. Originally located inside a large temple hall, the temple was destroyed and rebuilt multiple times after typhoons and a tidal wave during the fourteenth and fifteenth centuries. Since 1495, the Great Buddha has been sitting out in the open, in the lotus position, on the ground by some trees. His peaceful expression, combined with the backdrop of forested hills, creates a truly alluring and spectacular sight of cordiality and sincerity.

Whenever I needed a place to escape the pressures of work, worries, and stress, I took a day trip to Kamakura on the weekends. I enjoyed taking long walks in silence around the town, relaxing, praying, and contemplating everything that I was going through. Most people there spoke Japanese while exploring and shopping, which created a beautiful symphony of unfamiliar sounds. Not understanding the language allowed me to immerse myself deeply in a state of rest, adding to the charm of the experience. Being in Kamakura was always a spiritual experience of peace and gratitude, a great destination for finding relaxation away from the stresses of work and daily life.

8. The Grand Sumo Tournament: A Lesson in Tradition and Discipline

In the midst of Tokyo's scorching summer heat, I stumbled upon the Grand Sumo Tournament and found it to be the perfect way to release the stress of a busy workweek. Sumo wrestling is a traditional Japanese style of wrestling and the country's national sport. It's a full-body-contact competitive sport where two huge wrestlers face off, each attempting to force the other to step out of the ring or to touch the ground with any part of their body other than the bottoms of their feet. With bouts lasting only a few seconds, the sport showcases the wrestlers' strength, self-discipline, focus, upper-body skills, leg and hip movements, and balance.

The ring, built on top of a heavy platform, is about fifteen feet in diameter and is made of clay covered with sand. The roof above the ring is modeled after those used on Shinto shrines since sumo wrestling originated in ancient times as a performance to entertain the Shinto deities. Many traditional rituals in sumo wrestling are linked to the Shinto religion, such as the purification ritual of sprinkling salt around the ring before each match.

The life of a sumo wrestler is tough; they train from a young age and live in a special training camp known as a Heya. Their daily lives, including their strength training, sleep, diet, dress, character, manners, and self-discipline, are dictated by the strict traditions of sumo wrestling. Sumo wrestlers don't have maximum weight guidelines, and weight gain is an essential part of their training. Sumo wrestlers can easily find themselves matched off against someone many times their size. However, the goal is not just to get big, but to get strong.

A good sumo wrestler will easily eat 10,000 calories a day more than the average man. Because it is difficult to gain weight on the traditional Japanese diet, sumo wrestlers must eat their own special type of food, called Chankonabe, which is essentially a thick stew served along with meat, vegetables, tofu, noodles, and rice. Drinking large amounts of beer with their meals is also part of the strategy to gain weight, and after eating, the wrestlers take a long nap to help the body store most of the calories as fat.

Sumo wrestlers are ranked according to the ancient system, with the highest-ranked wrestlers or grand champions called Yokozuna. The tournaments take place over six annual official tournaments, three of which are always held in Tokyo, and each tournament lasts for fifteen days.

As someone who had never seen live sumo wrestling before, I decided to attend the Grand Sumo Tournament, even though tickets were sold out in advance. I ended up getting a ticket for the last day, which is the most popular as it is the day the topmost wrestlers go head-to-head and the Grand Sumo Champion title is awarded. I was struck by the scene at the Kokugikan, the sumo stadium in Tokyo's Ryogoku District. The stadium was shaped and designed like a traditional Japanese shrine or temple—a light-green rooftop and surrounded by a large, dark-colored steel fence decorated with balloons and special ornaments.

Inside the stadium, I found myself among men and women of all ages, all focused on the live matches. The wrestlers were divided into two groups and wore diverse, beautiful traditional garments, such as thick silk belts and half aprons. The pre-match rituals, including the ring purification ceremony that dates back over 1,000 years, were fascinating to watch. The referee and sumo judges carefully watched the wrestlers for any violations, and the matches were intense and exciting to witness.

One of the most remarkable aspects of sumo wrestling is the humility and self-discipline demonstrated by the wrestlers. Despite their size and strength, they bow respectfully to the audience before and after each match, and to their opponents before and after the bout. They show gratitude to their coaches and mentors, and are always striving to improve themselves, both physically and mentally. They adhere to a strict code of conduct, including a prohibition against engaging in any form of violence outside of the ring, and they are expected to maintain high levels of integrity and honor in their personal and professional lives.

Overall, attending the Grand Sumo Tournament was a unique and memorable experience that allowed me to immerse myself in the rich traditions of sumo wrestling and to gain a deeper appreciation for the sport. It also taught me valuable lessons about humility, self-discipline, and respect, which are integral parts of the training and behavior expected from sumo wrestlers. These values can be applied in any aspect of life, including cross-cultural communication and leadership, and can help us become better individuals and team members.

The tournament showcased not only the wrestlers' physical strength, but also their mental toughness and the discipline required to compete at the highest level. The Grand Sumo Tournament was a perfect example of how Japan has maintained its cultural heritage while still embracing modernity, and it served as a reminder that it's possible to hold on to tradition while still moving forward.

Attending the Grand Sumo Tournament provided me valuable lessons that extended beyond the realm of sports. It not only deepened my appreciation for the rich traditions of sumo wrestling, but also broadened my understanding of Japanese culture. Witnessing the wrestlers' humility, self-discipline, and unwavering respect taught me the importance of embodying these values in my own life.

9. Discovering Japan: A Journey of Bonding and Unforgettable Memories

On my first business trip to Japan, I remember thinking that it would be the last time I would visit. Later, I recall waiting for a connecting train at the underground Tokyo metro station and wondering again if it would be my last time in beautiful Japan. I never thought I would be there more than twenty times, leading large and high-priority projects. Over the years, my experiences in Japan while working with amazing engineers and non-engineers from our local team and clients have expanded my personality, made me more socially confident, and shaped the person that I'm today.

Some years ago, during a winter month, my mother and I embarked on a journey of discovery and bonding in Japan that would create unforgettable memories. For my mother, this trip was particularly special as she had dreamed of visiting Japan since her childhood in a small village in India. She never imagined that she would one day make the journey accompanied by her own son as a personal tour guide. The joy and excitement on her face were apparent, and it was an experience that we both cherished deeply.

I always wanted to accompany my parents on a trip to Japan, the place that had inspired and taught me so much about life. I had grown to appreciate and love the culture and had learned so much professionally and personally there. My father and my sister had separately come to visit me in Tokyo, but I was always engaged in work activities. I couldn't really take time off to be with them.

The trip with my mother was a different situation. It was our short getaway vacation, the perfect leisure time to relax and enjoy life. As an experienced international traveler, I had learned to endure the discomforts that came with such journeys, but I was concerned about my mother's well-being on the long flight. I encouraged her to stay hydrated and to move around the cabin, and I showed her simple arm and leg stretches to prevent cramps and stiffness.

As we descended into Tokyo, I felt a rush of excitement and anticipation. Looking out the airplane window, we saw a breathtaking view of clear blue skies overhead and the ocean meeting the coast of Japan. The beauty was further amplified as we flew over the lush greenery of the Japanese countryside, rice fields stretching out into the distance.

From the moment we stepped off the plane after landing at Narita International Airport in Tokyo, we were swept up in the vibrant energy of Japan. It had been a long thirteen-hour flight from Chicago, and we were visibly exhausted and stressed. We made our way through the terminal towards Customs, and then we took the airport bus to one of the top five-star luxury hotels in the center of Shinjuku, a major business and entertainment district of Tokyo. It was a two-hour ride from the airport.

While on the bus, my mother was looking through the glass window to her right, seeing cars and passing rice fields, homes, and buildings before we entered Tokyo. I was staring through the front windows of the bus, reflecting on how far I had come and feeling, with tearful eyes, a sense of deep gratitude for having a chance to be a part of Japan.

We arrived at the hotel; a twenty-eight-floor tall, modern, light-brown concrete structure covered with large glass windows on all floors. As soon as we entered the hotel lobby, we were warmly greeted by the hotel staff who directed us to a receptionist area. The check-in process was quick and efficient. The staff was welcoming, polite, and spoke fluent English.

We went to our large two-bed room on a higher floor with a spectacular nightly view of the Shinjuku skyline of tall buildings. We were both thrilled to be staying in such a Japanese-styled luxurious hotel, and we knew that it was the perfect base for our adventures in Tokyo. We couldn't wait to explore all that the city had to offer, and we were grateful to have such a comfortable and stylish home base to return to each night.

I then made a quick phone call from the hotel room to one of my closest Japanese friends whom I had not seen in a year. I had informed him ahead of time that we were coming to visit Tokyo. Immediately, he picked up the phone and was so excited. He didn't wish to wait until the next day to see me and meet my mother. My mother, on the other hand, was really tired, and she just wanted to go to bed. Although I didn't want to leave my mother alone on her first night in Tokyo, at the same time I wanted to honor my friend's request for a quick face-to-face meet-up. Honoring relationships is a very important part of the Japanese culture.

After a conversation with my mother, she graciously agreed to stay by herself and sleep while I went out to meet with my friend near the hotel. So, I quickly got ready, put on my shoes and a winter coat, and left to see my friend. We met at our usual spot on the ground level of the Shinjuku railway station, near the entrance to a famous Japanese clothing store. According to Japanese custom, we casually greeted each other first with a bow, followed by a handshake, and then a hug. All of our unspoken thoughts, words, and feelings came together in a deep sense of gratitude for our continued friendship after a year-long wait.

We went for a walk to a nearby busy restaurant for a quick bite to eat and to catch up. We were both so happy and full of joy to meet one another again in person. It was a noisy restaurant, but we managed to catch up, hang out, laugh, and make jokes; I also gave him my gift. Afterwards, we went to one of the popular inexpensive Japanese soba-noodle places in Omoide Yokocho (Piss Alley). It was really dark and crowded with shoulder-to-shoulder seating. After a quick, delicious bowl of Japanese soba noodles, I bid farewell to my friend and made my way back to the hotel.

The next day, after a delicious breakfast at the hotel, my mother and I headed to the bustling Shinjuku railway station on foot. We purchased our tickets and took the train to Asakusa, a district known for its historic temples and shrines. It was a perfect clear, sunny day, and we were both excited to explore more of Tokyo.

As we walked through the busy streets of Asakusa, we were immediately struck by the contrast between the traditional and modern architecture. Our first stop was the famous Senso-ji Temple, one of the oldest and most popular Buddhist temples in Tokyo. The temple's vibrant red and gold colors, intricate architecture, and serene atmosphere left us in awe. As we walked through the entrance gate of the temple, we could immediately sense the spiritual and peaceful atmosphere. We saw people offering prayers, bowing, and clapping their hands, a traditional way to show respect and gratitude and to ask for blessings.

We walked through the Nakamise-dori, a vibrant shopping street lined with vendors selling traditional Japanese souvenirs and street food. We tried some freshly made rice crackers and bought some traditional souvenirs to take back home. As we strolled through the streets, we also took pictures with women and men dressed in beautiful kimonos, adding to our unforgettable experience in Tokyo. My mother was thrilled and excited; all day, she had a huge smile on her face and was taking in every moment.

From Asakusa, we went to Ginza, Tokyo's crown jewel in terms of being a shopping, dining, and entertainment area. We had lunch at an Indian restaurant. My mother had masala chai, and we both ate delicious vegetarian food. From there, we took the train to Shibuya, a vibrant district famous for its fashionable boutiques, cafes, and nightlife. We walked through the famous Shibuya Crossing, a busy pedestrian intersection known as the busiest crossing in the world. Watching the sea of people cross the street in perfect synchronization was truly a sight to behold. As the day came to an end, we headed back to the hotel to relax and unwind with a delightful dinner.

The next few days of our trip were filled with more exciting adventures. We took a day trip to Kamakura, a coastal town known for its historic temples and famous big Buddha statue.

We also visited Hakone, another beautiful destination over an hour's bullet-train ride outside of Tokyo, famous for hot springs and natural beauty; then we took a boat ride on Lake Ashinoko, located nearby Mount Fuji. Over the mountain via ropeway, we observed the spectacular views of Owakudani's sulfur fields. We ended up using trains, ropeways, boats, and buses to get around the beautiful Hakone area. We also visited the Imperial Palace in Tokyo, which was a peaceful and serene escape from the busy streets of the city.

I also took my mother to see the company building where I worked, and we ended up having coffee and snacks at one of the best five-star international hotel brands in Tokyo, where I always stayed on my business trips. It was a proud moment of achievement for me as she looked around the hotel lobby and recognized all my hard work and sacrifices in Japan.

Overall, our trip to Tokyo was an unforgettable experience filled with exciting adventures, cultural experiences, and amazing moments of bonding between my mother and me. It was a trip that we will always remember and cherish.

Conclusion

As I come to the end of this book, I cannot help but feel overwhelmed with gratitude for the journey that has brought me to this moment. From humble beginnings to adapting to new environments and traveling the world, I have been blessed with experiences that have shaped my character, my outlook on life, and my appreciation for the people around me.

Through every obstacle, every hardship, and every success, I have learned the true value of resilience, perseverance, and the unwavering support of those closest to me. These lessons have taught me to never compromise my authenticity, to never back down from a challenge, and to always remain true to myself and continue making progress.

I'm eternally grateful for the love and support of my family, friends, mentors, and even strangers, who have offered their prayers, blessings, guidance, and encouragement throughout my journey. They have helped me move through adversity, find strength in difficult times, and shape the person I'm today. I owe them everything.

From my childhood adventures to my travels across the world, I have learned the importance of taking risks, embracing new experiences, and finding meaning. Navigating life requires a delicate balance of playfulness and seriousness, and a willingness to make mistakes and learn along the way.

Through the ups and downs of life, I have learned that perseverance, embracing change, building resilience, and a strong support system are essential. Whether it was navigating a new environment or dealing with professional or personal struggles, having people to lean on and offer guidance was crucial.

I have also come to appreciate the importance of taking care of my own physical and mental well-being. Whether it was taking time to rest and recharge during work or prioritizing my own self-care in the midst of challenging times, I have learned that being healthy and taking care of oneself is crucial to navigating life's obstacles.

My hope is that through my experiences, you have gained a greater sense of the resilience and strength we all possess within us. Life is full of ups and downs, but it's our ability to adapt, learn, and grow that helps us to navigate the challenges; only in that way can we emerge stronger on the other side.

I encourage you to embrace new experiences, whether through traveling for personal or business reasons, taking on international jobs and roles, immersing yourself in different cultures, making friends, and actively learning about the world; and by applying the lessons from my story to your own journey. Hopefully, like me, you too will gain something valuable to enrich your life journey.

I'm excited about the future and the journey ahead. I know that the lessons I have learned will continue to shape my perspective and guide me. Thank you for joining me on this journey, and I hope that my story has touched your heart.

Acknowledgments

Writing a book is harder than I thought and more rewarding than I could have ever imagined. None of this would have been possible without the support and encouragement of my friends, Dean Su, Anindya Sen, and Tony Roy. They were the first friends with whom I talked about writing a book; they helped review early drafts and gave me valuable feedback. They motivated me to write my stories and share them with the world. I deeply appreciate their support and friendship.

Special thanks to Lisa Umina, CEO of Halo Publishing, for believing in my story, providing invaluable guidance throughout the book-writing process, and helping to shape the vision for the book. I'm also grateful to my editor, Una Chester, for her crucial feedback and input that helped shape my writing. My appreciation also goes to the amazing team at Halo Publishing, including Fernanda Ramirez for her guidance and support, and Raul Medrano for designing a beautiful book cover. Thank you all for being a part of this journey with me.

I'm eternally grateful to my parents, Vipin and Bhagwati, for their love and support throughout my life. They worked tirelessly to provide for my sister and me, instilling in us the values of hard work and perseverance. They have always been so proud of our achievements. My mother, Bhagwati, has been a constant source of inspiration, teaching me the importance of humility, integrity, kindness, and relationships. Her selflessness and generosity have had a lasting impact on how I live my life. I'm forever thankful for my parents' blessings and guidance.

I also want to express my gratitude to my sister, Rinku, who has been my constant supporter throughout my life. Her love and encouragement have helped me navigate the challenges. I'm truly blessed to have her as my sister. Additionally, my heartfelt thanks to my brother-in-law, Abel, and my wonderful nieces, Nia and Bella, for their support.

My maternal and paternal grandparents (Ba and Dada) played instrumental roles in shaping who I'm today. They instilled in me the values of devotion, respect, service, and commitment that have guided me throughout my life. From listening to their stories of overcoming adversity, to watching them demonstrate unconditional love and support for family, they taught me invaluable lessons about resilience, empathy, and the importance of family. I have immense gratitude for their blessings and wisdom.

My maternal uncle, Prakash, and my aunts Vilas, Daxa, Bhavna, Nayana, and Bharti have played significant roles in shaping my childhood memories. Growing up, they were constant sources of fun and family time. From special celebrations to family dinners, they always made sure that our family bond remained strong. I'm so thankful for their love, generosity, and support throughout my life.

I'm grateful to my first boss, Raj Baxi, for taking a chance on me after college and for mentoring me and putting me in a position to succeed at work and on projects in Japan. He encouraged me to take on challenges and always reminded me of my potential. I cannot thank you enough for your support.

I would like to give my deep appreciation to my former coworker, Mitch Bratland, for his invaluable contribution to my success on various projects in Japan. He ensured that I received timely updates, and his coordinated daily conference calls on project issues were crucial to our success. Thank you for your friendship and support over the years.

I'm deeply grateful for the friendship and support of my former coworkers Rajesh Dave and Jaymin Patel. Rajesh and I spent most of our careers together in the same office, working on numerous telecom projects and sharing many meaningful conversations and afternoon walks. Jaymin has been there for me, encouraging me to follow my passion. I'm incredibly thankful for their friendship over the years.

I'm grateful to my former colleagues and clients in Japan, who have played pivotal roles in my success. While the list is long, I would like to acknowledge Sugiyama-san, Murata-san, Shizawa-san, Wada-san, and Hotta-san from our former Japan team, and Nomi-san and Miwa-san from our client's team. Our relationships have evolved from professional to personal, and I'm grateful for their friendship and support, which have helped me grow both personally and professionally.

I want to express my sincere gratitude to my friends from Japan, whose stories and experiences are featured in this book. Your friendship and support have meant the world to me. From sharing meals and laughter, to exploring places, thank you for memories that transcend cultural boundaries.

I'm grateful for the guidance and support of all the teachers who have helped me to learn and grow throughout my life. Without them, I may never have reached my full potential.

I'm deeply grateful to my friends from high school and college for their unwavering support, and the moments of laughter and fun we shared. Our shared experiences of empathy and understanding during challenging times have been invaluable.

Finally, I would like to sincerely express my gratitude to the readers who have taken the time to read my book. Your support and interest mean the world to me, and I'm honored to have shared my story with you. Thank you for embarking on this journey with me.

Finally, I would like to express my gratitude to God for everything!

About the Author

Nilesh V. Patel is a world traveler and cultural explorer who believes in embracing diversity, valuing traditions, and cultivating a positive attitude towards challenges. With extensive work and business experience across different cultures, he has learned valuable lessons in resilience and adaptability. As the founder of A Daily Happy, Nilesh inspires people around the globe to cultivate inner wisdom and happiness. Additionally, as the founder of the nonprofit organization Village Classroom, he is dedicated to providing education to underprivileged children in remote villages worldwide. Nilesh's vision and commitment to social impact make him a unique and inspiring figure in the world of personal development, and his experiences and stories about cross-cultural work in Japan provide a valuable perspective on challenges, relationships, and success.

www.ingramcontent.com/pod-product-compliance
Lightning Source LLC
Chambersburg PA
CBHW072138090426
42739CB00013B/3219